Secrets of the Turkish Kitchen

Illustrated by Sarah Carter
Cover design & Layout: Kapsam Grafik

Printed at Mart Matbaacılık Sanatları
Mart Plaza, Merkez Mah. Ceylan Sok.
No: 24 Nurtepe
Istanbul, Turkey
Tel: +90212 321 23 00

Published by:
Çitlembik Publications
Şeyh Bender Sokak 18/4 Asmalımescit
Tünel 80050 Istanbul / Turkey
Tel: +90212 292 30 32 / 252 31 63
Fax: +90212 293 34 66
www.citlembik.com.tr / kitap@citlembik.com.tr

Library of Congress Cataloging-in-Publication Data

Mitchell, Angie
    Secrets of the Turkish Kitchen /Angie Mitchell.-2nd ed.-İstanbul:
    132 p.-(Çitlembik Publications; 96)
    Includes index.
    ISBN : 975-6663-63-4
1.Cookery, Turkish.- 2.Cookery, Mediterranean
I.Title
LC:TX725.T8
DC:641.59561

Secrets of the Turkish Kitchen

Angie Mitchell

Illustrated by Sarah Carter

Angie Mitchell first came to Turkey in 1988 to pursue a career in the yachting industry. The beauty of the country, culture and its people were enough to convince her she would eventually make Turkey her home.

Great breaks offered her many adventures to explore the world under sail, and working as a chef provided excellent opportunities to discover various cultures and new cuisines.

Returning to Turkey in 1996, she spent time broadening her knowledge of Turkish cuisine and has now decided to share her newfound knowledge. Her book, Secrets of the Turkish Kitchen, represents a tribute to the country that has made her feel so much at home.

Author's acknowledgements

More than thanks go to Sarah Carter – her colourful illustrations portray Turkey in a bold and vibrant way, typifying the cuisine and giving the book life and soul. Heather, my mum, without whom I wouldn't have learned to love and respect food or realised my potential as a curious cook. Ali, Engin and Deniz İrengün - all our long discussions and exchanges about recipes, cooking methods and Turkish food culture have been invaluable. Annie Onursan in the UK and Karen of Amber Travel in Kaş for their dedication in trying and testing recipes. And, of course, the great friends who offered their services as proof readers – Helen Ford, Cathy Crawford and Christine Davies. Also Kim of SJ Travel and Chris Drum; their generosity, advice and support will never be forgotten. Last, but by no means least, the boys at Kapsam Grafik – Salih, Tolga and Suat. Nancy at Çitlembik for realising the vision, John Scott at Cornucopia for putting me in touch with her and Faith Hentschel and Fatih for keeping me independently mobile. Of others who have contributed in some way, however small, the list is endless. During my travels throughout Turkey, for those I've worked with, eaten with, cooked for, or have been just great, supportive friends – many, many thanks.

Elements of Turkish cuisine, glossary and global interpretations

Ayran – a drink made from yogurt and water with a pinch of salt

Bakla – broad bean, horse bean or fava bean

Bal – honey

Balkabağı – orange pumpkin

Beyaz peynir – white cheese made from sheep or cow's milk, referred to globally as feta cheese

Börek – the generic term for savoury pastries and pies

Bulgur – a grain made from cracked wheat berries, can be found in fine and coarse varieties

Çamfıstığı – pine nut kernels or pignolia

Çay – tea, harvested in the Black sea region

Cezve – a long-handled pot required for making Turkish coffee

Çörekotu – nigella, a small aromatic seed sometimes incorrectly referred to as black cumin

Dolma – generic term for anything with a stuffing

Et suyu – meat stock or broth/bouillon

Güveç – earthenware or terracotta pot used to make casseroles

Kabak – summer squash, courgette or zucchini

Kereviz – celeriac or celery root

Kahve – Turkish coffee

Kaşar peyniri – hard pale yellow cheese made from sheep or cow's milk. Can be substituted with mild cheddar

Kaymak – clotted cream made from water buffalo milk

Kırmızı biber – a type of chilli pepper originally from South America. Available from sweet and mild to ferociously hot

Kıyma – minced or ground meat, sometimes referred to as hamburger in the United States

Köfte – term for meat or vegetables shaped into a ball

Kuşüzümü – small black currant, sometimes referred to as bird grape

Maydanoz – flat leaf parsley

Mercimek – lentils

Meze – appetiser, small portion

Mısır nişantası – cornflour or cornstarch

Nar – pomegranate

Nar ekşisi – syrup made from sour pomegranates

Nohut – chickpeas or garbonzo beans

Patlıcan – aubergine or eggplant

Pastırma – air-dried fillet of beef coated in a combination of spices, similar to pastrami

Pekmez – boiled and concentrated grape juice used as a sweetening agent. Can also be found made from mulberries, dates and carob

Pilav – a pilaf or rice dish

Pudra şeker – powdered sugar, icing sugar or confectioners' sugar

Pul biber – paprika flakes

Sakız – mastic gum, used to flavour and thicken sweets. Highly prized by the Ottoman court

Salça – concentrated rich tomato paste, tomato puree

Semiz otu – purslane, also known as lamb's lettuce

Sucuk – heavily spiced and seasoned sausage

Sumak – dried berry of the sumac tree. Usually used in its ground form to give a tangy citrus taste

Tahin – an oily paste made from crushed sesame seeds, sometimes known globally as tahini

Tarator – a sauce made with ground nuts, garlic, bread, oil and vinegar

Tava – refers to a frying pan or fried dish

Tepsi – refers to a tray or baking tray used for making pastries

Terbiye – a mix of lemon, flour and eggs added to a dish to flavour and thicken

Un – plain white flour, white all-purpose flour

Yufka – thin, round sheets of ready-made pastry, which measure 60cm/2ft in diameter. Filo/phyllo can be used as a substitute

Zeytin – olive

Zeytinyağı – olive oil

Zeytinyağlı – generic term for the method of cooking or vegetable dishes cooked with olive oil

Explanatory notes

Weights, volumes and measures –

Throughout the book you will note the use of spoons and cups. You will rarely find scales being used in a Turkish kitchen and accuracy to the last grain is not an issue. Using cups and spoons therefore means cooking up a Turkish feast can become as low-maintenance as possible and using this book enjoyable and fun.

- 1 teaspoon - 5ml
- 1 tablespoon -15ml
- 1 cup - 250ml

Here are some more approximate guidelines to help things along, but keep in mind a few grams here and there will not affect the final result dramatically. Appreciate your own creative licence to add as little or as much seasoning, spices and herbs as you personally prefer. In recipes requiring rice, be aware different varieties may require slightly different cooking times and varying amounts of cooking fluid.

1 cup –
- grains, pulses, dried legumes, sugar = 200g/7-8oz
- stock, water, olive oil, yogurt, milk = 250ml/8-9floz
- flour, chopped nuts, dried fruit = 150g/5-6oz

1 tablespoon –
- grains, pulses, dried legumes, sugar = 15g / 1/2oz
- stock, water, olive oil, melted butter, yogurt, milk= 20g / 1/4oz
- flour, chopped nuts, dried fruit, spices = 10g/just under 1/2oz

- 1 onion = 150g/5-6oz

Unless otherwise stated throughout this book –

- All cheeses are full fat and unpackaged
- All milk is full fat
- All yogurt is full fat, live and free of sweeteners, thickeners or additives (if Turkish yogurt is unavailable, Greek yogurt can be substituted)
- All eggs are medium and organic/free-range
- All olive oil is extra virgin, anything too robust may effect the overall flavour
- All flour is all-purpose plain white flour. Stronger flour may be preferred for the dough recipes using yeast
- All rice is white, long grain. In Turkey premium baldo is the rice of choice. Precooked rice should be avoided as it is void of nutrients, texture and flavour
- All vegetables and fruit are organic and supplied by local farmers' markets
- All herbs used are fresh, parsley is of the flat-leafed variety
- All meat and chicken is provided by local butchers and is organic when possible
- All fish and seafood is freshly caught and supplied by local fishermen and fishmongers who should be delighted to clean and prepare the catch to your specifications

Contents

Introduction

Turkish cuisine is unique. The Anatolian peninsula has the combined characteristics of three continents: Europe, Africa and Asia. Surrounded by three different seas, the geographical, ecological and climatic diversity provides fertile lands. For millennia, many civilizations have fought for it and made it their home. Hittite, Roman and Byzantine dynasties all coveted this soil. Turkey today is one of the few countries in the world which can successfully feed its own population and have surplus to trade. Turkish cuisine reflects the diversity of its landscape, a rich cultural heritage and the dynamic resources of all its inhabitants, past and present.

In the 6th century nomadic tribes of Turkish origin migrated west from regions of central Asia and Mongolia. Their diet centred around their horses and herds, rich in meat and dairy. They were known as warriors and developed a deep sense of survival. They accumulated culinary influences from various Asian ethnic groups, the Chinese primarily, and adapted them to suit their nomadic lifestyle. During the 10th century they brushed shoulders with Persians and Arabs and were introduced to rice, lentils, new fruits and nuts. By the 11th century their wandering began to cease and for many tribes Anatolia was to become a permanent resting place. Here they planted crops, learning much from the indigenous inhabitants. They found new and varied produce and Anatolia's strategic position strengthened an emerging need to dominate this bountiful region. Their heritage as traders made it possible to control trade along the ancient silk routes, giving them access to even more exotic spices and ingredients. In 1453 various Turkish clans joined forces to form the new and imposing Ottoman strength which ultimately toppled the great walls of Constantinople, ending an era of Byzantine domination. The new and indulgent Ottoman supremacy employed scores of chefs. Huge palace kitchens were developed and designed to cater for massive state banquets; food became of major importance and the whims of sultans demanded new gastronomic heights. Different ethnic groups living within the Ottoman Empire were also to make an impression, and exciting produce such as tomatoes and peppers arrived from the Americas. Having absorbed much from ancient civilizations and now heirs to Anatolia's heterogeneous culture, the Turks still remained in touch with their own distinctive culinary identity. This synthesis manifests today as Türk mutfağı – Turkish cuisine, a hybrid fusion of fresh and natural ingredients and a result of immense and historic diversity.

The emphasis of Turkish cuisine is on seasonal freshness. Seasons herald new and tempting produce; tempo changes and different eating habits emerge according to the time of the year. Dishes are prepared in an uncomplicated way to produce a nutritionally balanced meal taking into account harmony of flavours and dietary requirements.

Today in Turkey, food and mealtimes are still the hub of everyday life. Seldom is food eaten 'on the hoof' and time is taken to share meals with family members or friends to relax and enjoy conversation. Always the participants wish each other 'afiyet olsun', literally meaning, may you be healthy. This is followed by a tribute to the creator of the meal, 'elinize sağlık', meaning health to your hands. Guests are always received with the highest cordial hospitality and it is believed no one should ever leave a Turkish table without feeling satisfied and happy.

Meze ve Salatalar

Appetisers and Salads

One of the most appealing aspects of dining in Turkey is a *meze* feast, a continuous stream of little plates adorned with mouthwatering appetizers, tasty dips and salads. Traditionally *meze* is accompanied with the nation's favourite tipple *rakı*, an anise flavoured spirit with the kick of a donkey.

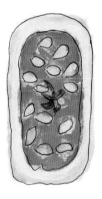

Meze counterparts are found throughout the Mediterranean and the Middle East, a trend which really caught on during the days of Ottoman supremacy. The word *meze* is of Persian origin, literally means 'enjoyable, pleasant taste' and is probably derived from the Arabic word 'mesaq'. During the opulent reign of Süleyman the Magnificent (1520-66), food tasters (*çeşnici*) became necessary to protect the sultan. Well known for his lavish and indulgent banquets, the palace chefs were ordered to prepare small portions of food for sampling. The palace created a tradition which soon became fashionable with the upper classes of Istanbul. As new and exotic foods became available the practice of serving experimental new dishes in small portions developed.

Today, *meze* can be served as an entrée, something to whet the appetite before the main course, or a range of specialities from the various regions of Turkey, constituting a meal in itself.

Kısır

Spicy bulgur wheat salad

Kısır is a speciality in the southeast of Turkey, from where the country's more spicy dishes hail. It is offered as a welcome to guests in the homes of Antakya and Gaziantep, where it is generally made with *nar ekşisi* (sour pomegranate syrup) instead of lemon juice. It can be rolled into balls and served nestling in crunchy lettuce leaves. This dish is perfect for buffets or as part of a barbecue spread.

Serves 4 - 6
Preparation time - 40 minutes

2 cups fine bulgur wheat	**juice of 1/2 lemon or**
1 1/2 cups boiling water	**1 tablespoon sour pomegranate syrup**
1 tablespoon tomato paste	**4 tablespoons olive oil**
1 teaspoon paprika paste	**4 spring onions, finely chopped**
1 teaspoon paprika flakes	**3 tomatoes, peeled and finely chopped**
1/2 teaspoon ground cumin	**handful of finely chopped parsley**
1 teaspoon salt	**handful of finely chopped mint**
freshly ground black pepper	**lettuce leaves to serve**
	lemon wedges to squeeze over

Put the bulgur in a bowl and add the boiling water. Leave to stand for 20 minutes. Most of the water should be absorbed. Drain and squeeze out any excess water if necessary. The bulgur should be of a dry consistency.

Stir in the tomato and red pepper pastes, paprika flakes, cumin, salt and freshly ground black pepper and knead thoroughly. Add the lemon juice or pomegranate syrup together with the olive oil and knead well again. Stir in the remaining ingredients and combine thoroughly.

Serve as a salad in a bowl garnished with lettuce leaves. Alternatively, take spoonfuls of the mixture and with wet hands roll into balls the size of walnuts. Refrigerate until required.

Serve on a platter with crispy fresh lettuce leaves and lemon wedges to squeeze over.

Note - Bulgur wheat, unlike cracked wheat, is a grain made from cooked wheat berries which have the bran removed, and are then dried and pounded. There are two varieties generally available, fine and coarse. Because it is pre-cooked it only requires a minimal amount of cooking to reconstitute itself.

Patlıcan Ezmesi

Smoked puréed aubergine with garlic and yogurt

To get the authentic smoked aubergine taste, it is essential to cook the aubergines over a charcoal grill, a gas flame or in a hot oven until their glossy skins are charred and blistered and the inner flesh is tender. In this recipe the flesh is then chopped and combined with garlic, lemon juice, oil and yogurt. The omission of yogurt and addition of chopped tomatoes, onions and parsley makes another great salad option.

Serves 4 - 6
Preparation time - 40 minutes

4 large aubergines
4 garlic cloves, crushed with salt
juice of 1/2 lemon
2 tablespoons olive oil

2 tablespoons natural creamy yogurt
salt and freshly ground black pepper
sprigs of parsley for garnish
black olives for garnish

Cook the aubergines as recommended for about 30 minutes. Use their stems to turn and rotate them from time to time and cook until the skins are charred and blistered, and the flesh is tender.

When cool enough to handle, strip away the blackened skin. Roughly chop the soft inner flesh and put in a colander, allowing any bitter juices to drain away.

In a bowl, combine the aubergine, garlic, lemon juice, olive oil and yogurt. Season with salt and pepper and mash into the consistency of a purée. Alternatively blitz together in a food processor. Refrigerate until required.

Serve garnished with parsley sprigs and black olives accompanied with freshly baked crusty bread.

Note - Also known as eggplant, aubergines can tend to be bitter and tough if too large. Go for the medium sized ones with glossy skins.

Humus

Chickpea and sesame purée

Also known as garbanzo beans, chickpeas grow in abundance in Turkey. This meze is a combination of chickpeas, garlic and *tahin* (a paste of crushed and puréed sesame seeds) which together create a delicious and nutritious dip. If you prefer a smoother dip, you may choose to remove the skins of the chickpeas before whizzing them with the other ingredients. Toasted *pide* bread (Turkish flat bread) is the perfect accompaniment.

Serves 8
Preparation time - 10 minutes
Cooking time - 1 hour

11/2 **cups chickpeas, soaked in water overnight or**
2 cans of precooked chickpeas
1 teaspoon salt
6 tablespoons olive oil
juice of 2 lemons
6 garlic cloves, crushed with salt

1/2 teaspoon sugar
6 tablespoons tahin (sesame paste)
1/2 teaspoon ground cumin (optional)
1/2 teaspoon ground paprika (optional)
olive oil and paprika flakes to serve

In plenty of fresh water boil the pre-soaked chickpeas rapidly for 10 minutes. Reduce the heat and continue cooking until they are well cooked and nearly to the point of mushiness, approximately 60-90 minutes. Towards the end of cooking time add the teaspoon of salt.

Drain and reserve some of the cooking liquid. Whilst still hot, put the chickpeas in a food processor or, using a hand blender, blitz them together with the olive oil, lemon juice, garlic, sugar and tahin. If it appears thick and difficult to blend, add some of the reserved cooking liquid. Season with more salt if required and mix in the cumin and paprika if desired. Process until you achieve a soft, smooth paste. Refrigerate until required.

Serve in a bowl drizzled with olive oil and a scattering of paprika flakes together with hot toasted bread.

Note - Never cook pulses in the water they were soaked in as it contains indigestible sugars. Skimming off any scum that forms during cooking will also help combat any negative digestive effects.

Haydari

Mint and garlic yogurt dip

A typical meze spread is difficult to envisage without this classic yogurt dip. Easy to whip up, it just seems to compliment everything and goes together particularly well with hot spicy dishes. Ideally, it is made with *süzme yoğurt*, a thick strained yogurt. Dill can be used to replace the mint or you can use a combination of both.

Serves 4 - 6
Preparation time - 10 minutes

4 cups thick strained yogurt
4 garlic cloves, crushed with salt
1 tablespoon dried mint or
4 tablespoons fresh mint, finely chopped
squeeze of lemon juice

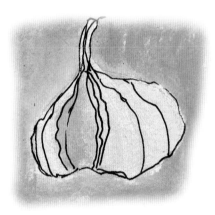

Combine all the ingredients in a bowl and mix well. Refrigerate until required.

Serve on a platter garnished with fresh mint leaves.

Note - To crush garlic quickly and effectively, use a pestle and mortar and add a little salt to work it into a smooth paste, allowing all the valuable oils to be released.

Acı Domates Ezmesi

Crushed chilli and tomato dip

This dip is a fiery little number and can be made in varying degrees of spiciness. The green pepper can be a hot or sweet one depending on how spicy you want the end result. *Nar ekşisi* (sour pomegranate syrup) can be used instead of lemon juice and fresh mint is also a preferable addition.

Serves 4 - 6
Preparation time - 15 minutes

6 tomatoes, peeled and finely chopped
1 small cucumber, grated
1 green pepper, finely chopped
4 spring onions, finely chopped
6 garlic cloves, crushed with salt
grated zest of 1 lemon
1 teaspoon paprika paste
1 tablespoon olive oil

juice of 1/2 lemon or
1 tablespoon sour pomegranate syrup
2 tablespoons tomato paste
handful of parsley, finely chopped
handful of fresh mint, finely chopped or
1 teaspoon dried mint
1/2 teaspoon sugar
salt and black pepper to taste

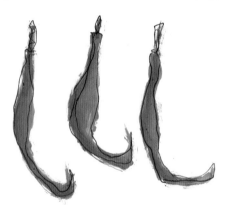

Place the tomatoes and cucumber in a sieve, sprinkle a little salt over and leave for 30 minutes to allow any excess water to drain away.

Combine all the ingredients in a bowl and mix well or blitz quickly in a food processor, taking care not to over pulverize. Chill in the fridge until required.

Garnish with fresh mint leaves and serve with freshly baked crusty bread.

Note - To remove the skins of tomatoes easily, pierce with a fork through the stalk end, cut a cross shape through the skin at the opposite end and immerse in boiling water for 10 seconds. Rinse under cold water and peel away the skin.

Fasulye Piyazı

Haricot bean salad

This dish has reached acclaim in Istanbul's famous *köfteci* establishments, as being the only true accompaniment to great meatballs. Accompanied with a refreshing glass of *ayran*, it has to be one of the most nourishing lunches around.

Serves 4 - 6
Preparation time - 20 minutes
Cooking time - 1 hour

1 1/2 cups dried haricot beans, soaked in water
overnight
or 2 cans precooked beans
1 teaspoon salt
1/2 cup olive oil
juice of 1 lemon
3 tomatoes, peeled and roughly chopped
1 large onion, halved and thinly sliced

1/2 cup chopped parsley
(dill and mint may be used)
1/2 teaspoon paprika flakes (optional)
salt and freshly ground black pepper to taste
2 hardboiled eggs, quartered
1/2 cup black olives, halved and stones removed
extra sprigs of parsley, for garnish

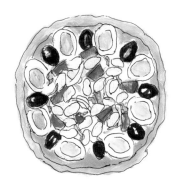

Drain the beans and put in a pan with plenty of fresh water. Cook for about 60 minutes or until tender, adding the salt towards the end of cooking time. Drain and set aside in a bowl.

Whisk together the olive oil and lemon juice and pour over the warm beans. Add the chopped tomatoes, onion and parsley, and paprika if desired. Season with salt and freshly ground black pepper and combine well. Arrange on a serving platter or in a bowl and garnish with the eggs, olives and sprigs of parsley.

Serve immediately or refrigerate until required.

Note - If you are short of time the overnight soaking process for beans can be speeded up. First cook the beans for 2 minutes in boiling water, remove from the heat and then leave them soaking in this water for a further 2 hours. Drain, rinse and using fresh water, continue the normal cooking procedure.

Sarımsaklı Havuç

Carrots with a garlic infused yogurt dressing

Always a favourite, this is carrots at their tastiest, dressed to kill with garlic infused yogurt. This dish also works well using beetroot or courgettes. Serve anytime, anywhere, but it always goes down particularly well al fresco, as a meze or salad accompaniment to grilled meats straight from the barbecue.

Serves 4 - 6
Preparation time - 20 minutes
Cooking time - 5 minutes

450g/1lb carrots, peeled and coarsely grated
2 tablespoons olive oil
1 teaspoon salt
1/2 teaspoon sugar
250g/9oz natural, thick and creamy yogurt
2 garlic cloves, crushed with salt
sprigs of parsley for garnish
paprika flakes for garnish

In a deep frying pan, over a low heat, lightly sauté the carrots in the olive oil. Add the salt and sugar, cook them down to half their original volume, still retaining their crunchiness, and set aside to cool.

Whisk together the yogurt and the garlic until smooth and creamy.

Transfer the carrots to a glass serving bowl and when cool, pour the yogurt over. Alternatively, stir the yogurt into the carrots and serve on a platter. Refrigerate until required.

Serve garnished with sprigs of parsley and a sprinkling of paprika flakes.

Note - Carrots are amazing: one carrot will supply enough vitamin A for an entire day and is reputed to cut down the risk of cancer. Carrots should be prepared just before use to maximise their valuable nutrients.

Cacık

Yogurt with cucumber and garlic

Some of the finest yogurt in the world is made in Turkey. Yogurt is an important feature of the Turkish diet, and is included in some way at most family meal times. Cacık is not so much a meze but more a chilled yogurt soup. It is easy to whisk up, and served in a small bowl alongside hot meat dishes, to refresh and cleanse the palate. If you wish, exclude the water and ice to create a great cooling dip. Add as much garlic as you like!

Serves 4 - 6
Preparation time - 10 minutes

500g/2 cups of natural, creamy yogurt
2 garlic cloves, crushed with salt
2 cucumbers, peeled, seeds removed and grated
2 tablespoons chopped fresh mint or
1 tablespoon dried mint
salt to taste
drizzle of olive oil
fresh mint leaves to garnish
water and ice cubes to serve

Combine the yogurt and garlic and beat until smooth. Stir in the grated cucumber and mint. Add salt to taste and then ice cold water to the desired consistency. Refrigerate until required.

Serve in bowls with a few ice cubes and add fresh mint leaves for garnish. (If using ice cubes take care not to add too much water in the preparation stage).

Note - Praised for its health-giving qualities, yogurt is rich in calcium, phosphorus and B vitamins and has earned a reputation as one of the most valuable health foods. The bacteria in live yogurt are known to stimulate friendly bacteria in the gut, easing gastrointestinal problems and aiding digestion.

Fava

Broad bean purée

Broad beans were first cultivated by the ancient Egyptians and variations of this dish can be found throughout Turkey and the Middle East. As with most legumes, they are packed with protein, vitamins, minerals and fibre, and they are extremely low in fat. This recipe uses the dried variety, but fresh beans work just as well, in which case the outer skin of the bean is discarded to create a smoother paste. Traditionally in Turkey, it is served in with a sprinkling of fresh dill in order to ease digestion.

Serves   8
Preparation time - 15 minutes
Cooking time - 40 minutes

2 cups dried broad beans, soaked in cold water overnight or 3 cups fresh broad beans
2 onions, quartered
1 carrot, peeled and cut into chunks
1 medium size potato, peeled and cut into chunks
6 whole garlic cloves
1/2 cup olive oil

2 teaspoons salt
2 teaspoons sugar
extra salt and freshly ground pepper to taste
olive oil to drizzle
paprika and chopped fresh dill to garnish
lemon wedges to squeeze over

Drain the soaked beans and discard any remaining dark outer skins. Place them in a pan with the onions, carrot, potato, garlic, olive oil, salt and sugar. Add enough water to cover (about 3 cups), and simmer for about 45 minutes or until all the ingredients are mushy and most of the cooking liquid is absorbed. Stir occasionally, skim off any scum that may rise to the surface and add more water during the cooking time if required.

Remove from the heat, allow to cool a little then blitz the mushy mixture with a hand blender or in a food processor. Alternatively, mash well and press through a sieve with a wooden spoon. The mixture should be a creamy, thick pouring consistency. Season with a little more salt and freshly ground black pepper if required.

Pour into a well oiled mould or bowl, cover and refrigerate overnight, allowing the fava to set.

Turn out the fava onto a serving plate (you may need to put the bowl briefly in boiling water to allow the fava to ease out gently). Drizzle with olive oil, sprinkle with freshly chopped dill and paprika and serve with lemon wedges to squeeze over. Enjoy with freshly toasted bread.

Patates Köftesi

Crispy potato and cheese croquettes

Generally served hot as part of a meze spread, these versatile croquettes can be prepared in advance and kept in the fridge or freezer until required and then thrown in hot oil to serve within minutes. They are also a great accompaniment for most meat dishes and a great hit with children. Any cheese can be used, but a mature hard cheese works best.

Serves 4 - 6
Preparation time - 15 minutes
Cooking time - 45 minutes

1kg/2lbs potatoes
200g/8oz mature hard cheese, grated
1 egg, beaten
2 tablespoons plain white flour

salt and freshly ground black pepper to taste
freshly grated nutmeg
2 cups fine breadcrumbs
sunflower oil for shallow frying

Boil the potatoes whole in their skins for about 25-30 minutes or until soft. Drain and when cool enough to handle, peel away the skins.

In a large bowl, mash the potatoes until smooth. Add the cheese, beaten egg, flour, nutmeg, salt and pepper to taste and work into a smooth paste. Chill the mixture in the fridge for approximately 1 hour.

Sprinkle the breadcrumbs onto a large plate. Take a large tablespoon of the potato mixture at a time and roll into finger shaped croquettes with oily hands. Roll each one in the breadcrumbs. Refrigerate or freeze until required.

The croquettes can be deep-fried or shallow-fried in sunflower oil. In either case avoid overloading the pan, turn carefully to brown evenly on all sides and drain on absorbent kitchen paper.

Serve hot as part of a meze spread.

Note - The vitamins and minerals in potatoes are stored just beneath the skin. Discard any potatoes with green patches as these contain toxic alkaloids called solanines.

Mercimek Köftesi

Spicy red lentil balls

The humble lentil is one of the world's oldest foods. It originates from North Africa and Asia and came to Turkey via trading routes from Egypt. It continues to be a staple in most Turkish households. This dish combines red lentils with bulgur wheat to create a classic and tasty meze, found at most weddings and family reunions. Unlike most pulses, red lentils do not require soaking.

Serves 6
Preparation time - 20 minutes
Cooking time - 10 minutes

1 cup red lentils
1 cup fine bulgur wheat
1 onion, finely chopped or
6 spring onions, finely chopped
1 tablespoon tomato paste
1 teaspoon paprika
1 teaspoon cumin
1 cup parsley, finely chopped
salt and freshly ground black pepper to taste
lettuce leaves to serve
lemon wedges to serve

Rinse the lentils, put in a pan with 3 cups of water and cook over a medium heat for 10 minutes. Add the bulgur and continue cooking for a further 2 minutes. Remove from the heat and leave to stand for 20 minutes. The bulgur should absorb any surplus water.

When cool, add the onion, tomato paste, spices, chopped parsley and season with salt and pepper. Mix well to create a smooth paste and chill the mixture in the fridge for 1 hour.

With wet hands shape the mixture into balls the size of large walnuts and with your finger create a small indentation. Cover and refrigerate until required.

Serve on a generous bed of lettuce leaves decorated with lemon wedges. To eat, squeeze lemon juice into the indentations and roll up the köfte in a crunchy lettuce leaf.

Semizotu Salatası

Purslane salad in a yogurt and garlic dressing

Purslane – *portulaca oleracea*, grows in abundance in the summer months and is not only used as a salad vegetable but can be used to replace spinach in many hot dishes and stews. Its fleshy leaves are highly nutritious, a good source of vitamin C, calcium and iron.

Serves 4
Preparation time - 15 minutes

1 bunch/250g/8oz purslane
1 cup natural yogurt
2 cloves garlic, crushed in salt
olive oil to serve

Wash the purslane. Strip away the leaves from the stalks. Discard the thick stalks and any bruised or damaged leaves. Dry the remaining leaves on absorbent kitchen paper.

Crush the garlic with a little salt in a pestle and mortar. Add the garlic to the yogurt and beat until creamy.

To serve, put the purslane leaves in a salad bowl and pour the yogurt over. Drizzle with a little olive oil and toss gently.

Note - Spinach also combines excellently with yogurt. Steam or blanch the spinach until nicely wilted. Drain off any water; chop finely and then combine with garlicky yogurt as above.

Deniz Börülcesi

Samphire dressed in olive oil, lemon and garlic

Often thought to be seaweed, samphire grows wild in dried out salt marsh areas during the summer months. It makes an interesting meze and beautifully compliments other fish and seafood appetisers. It is extremely rich in vitamins and iron.

Serves 4 - 6
Preparation time - 15 minutes
Cooking time - 5 minutes

500g/1lb fresh samphire
juice of 1 lemon
2 cloves garlic, crushed
olive oil to dress

Boil the samphire in fresh water for 5 minutes or until tender. Do not add salt, it is salty enough. Strain and plunge into ice cold water to retain its vibrant green colour, taste and nutritional content.

When cool enough to handle strip the fleshy shoots from the inedible stalks. It should ease away easily between your thumb and forefinger.

To serve, toss together with the lemon juice and garlic and a little olive oil.

Note - Raw garlic is thought to relieve the symptoms of food poisoning.

Kabak Çiçeği Dolması

Stuffed courgette flowers

The hardy summer courgette graces the Turkish table in many wonderful forms. Its bright, yellow blooms open early in the morning and scream to be picked and stuffed. This delicately flavoured recipe is from the Bodrum peninsula.

Serves 4 - 6
Preparation time - 25 minutes
Cooking time - 40 minutes

20 courgette flowers
5 courgette leaves
1 cup rice
4 tablespoons olive oil
2 onions, finely chopped

1 teaspoon salt
2 tomatoes, skinned and finely chopped
juice of 1/2 lemon
1/2 cup of fresh dill and mint, finely chopped
lemon wedges to squeeze over

Soak the rice in hot salted water for 30 minutes. Drain and rinse thoroughly under running water.

Heat 2 tablespoons of olive oil, sauté the onion until soft and add the rice. Cook for 5 minutes and add the chopped tomato and salt. Add enough water to just cover the rice and continue cooking until the water is absorbed. Remove from the heat, cover with a cloth and replace the lid. Set aside to cool.

Remove the inner stamens of the flower, wash and drain on an absorbent kitchen towel.

In a bowl, combine the cooled rice with the chopped dill and mint. Carefully spoon the mixture into each flower, folding over the tops to encase the filling.

Line a pan with the courgette leaves and then pack the flowers tightly into the pan. Mix the remaining 2 tablespoons of olive oil with the lemon juice and 2 tablespoons of water. Pour this over the flowers, cover and cook over a medium heat for 30 minutes, or until the liquid is absorbed.

Serve at room temperature with lemon wedges to squeeze over.

Çorbalar
Soups

'Çorba' is deeply ingrained in Turkey's nomadic past. Classic Turkish soup is made with a meat stock, designed to make valuable use of the entire animal - heads, bones and offal. Combinations of pulses and grains, flavoured with herbs and spices make nourishing hearty soups. Lighter soups are thickened with egg and lemon (*terbiye*) and others sharpened with vinegar. *Tarhana* is probably Turkey's most symbolic soup; a mix of coarsely ground wheat and yogurt, pounded together with spices and tomato paste left in the hot summer sun to dry. The dried dough is then crumbled and stored indefinitely to provide instant soup. Shepherds use this as a food source during the months they spend with their flocks in remote mountain pastures.

During the Ottoman period soups held great significance. Soup kitchens were established outside the palace boundaries to feed the poor. Huge copper soup cauldrons also became of social importance for the elite Janissary regiments of the Ottoman army. In times of mutiny, cauldrons would be overturned to express their dissatisfaction with the sovereign power.

Soup can be the first course of a meal or be nourishing enough to be a meal in itself. It is drunk, not eaten and can be consumed at any time of the day. Soup can be breakfast, lunch or dinner.

Düğün Çorbası

Wedding soup

Traditionally a sheep may be slaughtered to honour the many guests invited to a wedding feast. This soup is popular at weddings and makes use of the neck of the sheep. It is served hot and drizzled with paprika butter.

Serves 8
Preparation time - 15 minutes
Cooking time - 1 hour 15 minutes

900g/2lbs neck of lamb or beef
1 onion, quartered
1 carrot, peeled and chopped
1 small celeriac, peeled and chopped
1 bunch of parsley, leaves and stalks separated
2 teaspoons salt
1 teaspoon whole black peppercorns

1 tablespoon wine vinegar
4 tablespoons plain white flour
4 tablespoons natural yogurt
juice of 1 lemon
2 egg yolks
4 tablespoons butter
1 teaspoon paprika flakes

Put the meat, vegetables, parsley stalks, salt and peppercorns in a large pan. Cover with water, add the vinegar, bring to the boil and simmer over a medium heat for an hour or until the meat is tender and falling away from the bones. Add more water during cooking time if necessary. Finely chop the parsley leaves and set aside for garnish.

Drain the stock through a sieve into another pan. When the bones are cool enough to handle, remove the meat. Shred it into small pieces and set aside. Press the remaining vegetables through the sieve into the stock, discarding the parsley stalks and peppercorns. Reheat the stock gently and set aside.

Mix together the flour, yogurt, lemon juice, egg yolks and beat until smooth. From the pan, take a cupful of hot stock and whisk it into the egg mixture. Gradually whisk in 3 more cupfuls of the stock.

Stir the thickened egg mixture gradually back into the pan of hot stock, add the shredded meat and simmer gently for 5 minutes. Adjust the seasoning if required, and add extra water if it seems too thick.

In a separate pan, melt the butter, add the paprika and cook gently for 30 seconds.

Serve the soup hot, drizzled with the paprika butter and a scattering of chopped parsley leaves, together with freshly baked bread.

Note - The vinegar is added to this soup to enable the bones to impart their valuble calcium and flavour to the stock.

İşkembe Çorbası

Hangover remedy tripe soup

An entire culture has grown up around tripe soup in Turkey and it is sold around the clock in the many soup kitchens. Believed to have a sobering effect, many Turks drink a steaming bowl of this soup, drizzled with garlic infused vinegar, after an evening of overindulgence. It is of course an acquired taste!

Serves 4 - 6
Preparation time - 15 minutes
Cooking time - 2 hours

450g/1lb cleaned lamb or veal tripe
6 cups/1 1/2 litres water
1/2 onion (left whole)
2 garlic cloves, roughly crushed
1 tablespoon wine vinegar
salt and freshly ground black pepper
1 egg yolk
juice 1/2 lemon
1 tablespoon plain flour

For the accompanying drizzle -
4 garlic cloves, crushed with salt
salt to taste
1/2 cup wine vinegar

Cut the tripe up into large pieces and put it with the water, onion, garlic and vinegar in a pan. Cover and cook slowly for 1 1/2 hours or until the tripe is tender. This may take longer and you may have to add more water during the cooking time.

Remove the tripe and strain the stock through a sieve into another pan, discarding the onion and garlic. When the tripe has cooled, cut into bite-size pieces.

Return the tripe to the stock, season with salt and pepper and simmer gently. Remove from the heat and set aside.

In a separate bowl, beat the egg yolk with a pinch of salt, lemon juice and flour, adding a little water if required. Into this egg mixture, stir half a cupful of the tripe stock and whisk thoroughly, adding a little more stock at a time.

Return the thickened egg mixture to the pan and return to a gentle heat. Continue stirring the soup as it thickens.

Using a pestle and mortar, crush the garlic with a pinch of salt and add to the vinegar.

Serve the soup hot with the optional drizzle of garlicky vinegar for that extra zing.

Kırmızı Mercimek Çorbası

Hearty red lentil soup

Because of their rich protein content, lentils have been a valuable food source in Asia Minor since Neolithic times. Lentil soup is probably Turkey's most popular soup today. You may even be offered it for breakfast on a cold winter's morning!

Serves 6
Preparation time - 10 minutes
Cooking time - 40 minutes

1 cup red lentils, rinsed and drained
1 tablespoon rice, rinsed and drained
1 large onion, quartered
1 large carrot, peeled and roughly chopped
1 litres/4 cups meat stock (stock cubes can be used)
2 tablespoons butter

salt and freshly ground black pepper
1 cup milk (optional)
2 tablespoons tomato paste (optional)
paprika flakes to serve (optional)
lemon wedges to serve (optional)
croutons to serve (optional)

Put the lentils, rice, onion, carrot and stock together in a pan. Bring to the boil and over a medium heat, simmer for about 30 minutes, or until the lentils and rice are well cooked. Stir occasionally to ensure the lentils don't stick to the bottom of the pan and skim off any scum that might float to the surface.

Traditionally, the soup is sieved to create a smooth consistency. Alternatively use a blender and blitz until smooth. Return the soup to the pan, add the butter and season with salt and pepper. If you prefer creamy soup, add the milk, or for a richer soup add the tomato paste. Mix well, return to the heat and add a little extra water if necessary to get the right consistency.

Serve hot with croutons and paprika flakes if desired. A squeeze of lemon juice adds an extra zing.

Ezo Gelin Çorbası

Daughter-in-law's soup

Tradition demands the new bride should win her mother in law's approval. Much depends on her abilities as a cook and this soup is the test. Named after the bride 'Ezo' who managed to impress her in-laws, it can be made with rice, but in more rural areas it is traditionally made with bulgur.

Serves 4 - 6
Preparation time - 5 minutes
Cooking time - 40 minutes

1/2 cup red lentils, rinsed and drained
1 onion, finely chopped
1 litre/4 cups meat stock (stock cubes can be used)
2 tablespoons rice/bulgur wheat, rinsed and drained
2 tablespoons tomato paste
4 tablespoons butter
salt and pepper to taste
1 teaspoon dried mint
1 teaspoon paprika flakes

Put the lentils, onion, stock, rice, water, tomato paste and butter together in a pan. Bring to the boil and then on a low heat simmer, stirring occasionally, for about 30 minutes until the lentils and rice are tender and the soup has a creamy consistency. Add more water if required and season with salt and pepper.

Add the paprika and mint and simmer for a further 5 minutes.

Serve hot with fresh crusty bread.

Balık Çorbası

Tangy fish soup

For this soup use any firm white fleshy fish. Whiting, gurnard and monkfish are ideal. The trick is to poach the fish whole to get the real Mediterranean fish flavour and then discard the head and bones. It's healthy and totally delicious!

Serves 4 - 6
Preparation time - 20 minutes
Cooking time - 20 minutes

450g/1lb whole fish of choice, cleaned and gutted
1/2 onion (left whole)
1 garlic clove, roughly crushed
2 bay leaves
1 teaspoon peppercorns
1 bunch parsley, stalks and leaves separated
1 bunch dill, stalks and leaves separated

6 cups/11/2 litres water
3 tablespoons olive oil
2 tablespoons plain white flour
juice of lemon
2 egg yolks
salt and freshly ground black pepper
lemon wedges for serving

Place the fish, onion, garlic, bay leaves, peppercorns, dill and parsley stalks (chop the leaves for use as garnish and set aside), water and a little salt in a pan. Poach gently for about 10 minutes or until the fish flakes easily from the bones. Try not to overcook, as this will lose valuable flavour.

Using a straining spoon, transfer the fish to a plate and set aside to cool. Strain the fish stock through a sieve into a clean pan, discarding the onion, peppercorns and herbs. When the fish is cool, peel the flesh away from the bones and add this to the fish stock. Reheat the stock gently and set aside.

In a separate bowl, beat together the olive oil, flour, lemon juice and egg yolks. Into this mixture stir half a cupful of the fish stock. Whisk thoroughly, slowly adding a little more stock. Return this mixture to the pan, season with salt and pepper and stir over a gentle heat as the soup thickens.

Serve garnished with a sprinkle of chopped parsley and dill, and lemon wedges to squeeze over.

Yayla Çorbası

Soup of the mountain pastures

This simple, but interesting yogurt based soup originates back to Anatolia's earliest settlers and nomadic herdsman. Today it is one of the country's most popular soups.

Serves 6
Preparation time - 10 minutes
Cooking time - 30 minutes

1 litre/4 cups of beef stock
(stock cubes can be used)
1/2 cup of rice, rinsed and drained
2 cups natural yogurt
2 tablespoons plain white flour

1 egg yolk
salt and freshly ground black pepper
4 tablespoons butter
4 teaspoons dried mint
paprika flakes to serve (optional)

Bring the stock to the boil and add the rice. Over a medium heat, simmer for about 20 minutes or until the rice is well cooked and has released its starch to thicken the soup. Remove from heat.

Meanwhile in a bowl, combine the yogurt, flour and egg yolk and beat until smooth. From the pan, take a cupful of hot stock and whisk it into the egg mixture.

Return the thickened egg mixture to the soup pan, season with salt and pepper and simmer gently for 5 minutes.

In a separate pan, melt the butter gently, add the mint and cook on a very low heat for 30 seconds. Whisk this butter into the soup.

Serve hot, topped with a sprinkling of paprika flakes.

Sebze Yemekleri

Vegetable Dishes

In Turkey vegetables are plentiful and regarded with passion. Village markets (*pazar*) supplied by local farmers are a constant bloom of vibrant colour, ripe and juicy tomatoes, cabbages too big to carry home and wild greens plucked freshly from the earth. Seasonal produce is dried, pickled and preserved to be enjoyed throughout the year.

Vegetables are always bought and prepared at their freshest, the most popular method being – *zeytinyağlı*. This method involves poaching the vegetable with a little water and olive oil, harnessing their natural flavour and nutritional value. Turks also love to stuff vegetables. In fact dolma – literally meaning stuffed, is the generic term for anything with a filling. Most characteristic of Turkish cuisine are stuffed green peppers and tomatoes; however many other vegetables and leaves find themselves hosts to fillings. Rich, red succulent tomatoes are an indispensable ingredient of the Turkish kitchen and salça, a concentrated tomato paste, is used in a wide number of dishes. But without doubt, the national vegetable has to be the aubergine; it makes an appearance in pies, pilafs and even pops up in jam.

Zeytinyağlı Taze Fasulye

Green beans, tomatoes and onions cooked with olive oil

Green beans cooked this way are a great national favourite. Enjoyed by urban and rural families alike, there are varying theories of how to achieve the best result. This is the most effortless way. Traditionally, *zeytinyağlı* dishes are prepared in advance and served at room temperature as a meze or vegetable course. French, runner and dwarf beans are all suitable to be prepared in this way.

Serves 4
Preparation time - 10 minutes
Cooking time - 25 minutes

500g/1.1lbs green beans
1 medium onion, finely chopped
1-2 tomatoes, skinned and chopped
4 tablespoons olive oil
1 cup hot water
salt and sugar to taste
lemon wedges to serve

Top, tail and string the beans, cut according to preference, or leave whole. Place in a pan with all the other ingredients.

Cover and cook over a medium heat for about 20 minutes or until tender. Remove from the heat and set aside to cool in the pan.

Transfer to a serving dish and serve with wedges of lemon to squeeze over.

Zeytinyağlı Enginar

Globe artichokes cooked with olive oil

Artichokes grow wild in Turkey. It is uncommon for them to be served with their leaves and the preparation involved to strip them down to their bare hearts is an effortless skill mastered in most homes. This recipe is well worth all the effort and pays tribute to this wonderful vegetable. Keep some of the stalk intact so they can be served proudly upside down with their stalks in the air.

Serves 4
Preparation time - 25 minutes
Cooking time - 20 minutes

4 globe artichokes,
(outer leaves and chokes removed)
6-8 spring onions, roughly chopped
1/4 cup olive oil
juice of 1/2 lemon
1/2 cup hot water
salt and sugar to taste
fresh dill for garnish
lemon wedges to serve

To prevent discolouration during the preparation, keep the raw artichokes in water with a squeeze of lemon juice.

Drain and place the artichokes, stalk side up, in a pan. Add the other ingredients, cover and on a medium heat cook gently for 20 minutes or until tender and most of the cooking liquid has been absorbed. Add a little finely chopped dill towards the end of cooking time.

Remove from the heat and set aside to cool in the pan.

Transfer to a serving plate, stalk side up. Drizzle with extra olive oil, garnish elegantly with sprigs of dill and serve with lemon wedges to squeeze over.

İmam Bayıldı

Tomato, onion and garlic stuffed aubergines

Literally translated, this dish is called 'The Priest Fainted'. It was one of the many *zeytinyağlı* dishes masterminded by chefs of the Ottoman palace kitchens. This dish obviously had the desired effect and hence was given such a dramatic name. There are said to be 40 recipes in Turkish cuisine using aubergine, and Turks are particularly passionate about it. Imam Bayıldı makes a great option as part of a light lunch.

Serves 6
Preparation time - 30 minutes
Cooking time - 60 minutes

6 medium aubergines, long thin variety   **salt and sugar to taste**
4 tablespoons olive oil   **juice of 1 lemon**
3 medium onions, finely chopped   **1/2 cup chopped parsley**
3 tomatoes, skinned and chopped   **1/2 cup hot water**
8 cloves of garlic, finely sliced

Preheat oven to 200c/400f/gas mark 6.

With a sharp peeler, partially peel the aubergines in alternate vertical stripes from stem to base, leaving the stalk intact. In each aubergine cut a deep slit lengthways, without cutting through to the skin on the opposite side, and leaving 1.5cm/1/2 in uncut at either end. Put the aubergines in a bowl of salted water for about 30 minutes, using a plate as a weight to hold them under the surface.

Heat some of the olive oil and sauté the chopped onions until translucent. Transfer the onions to a bowl with a slotted spoon and add the chopped tomatoes, garlic, salt, sugar, lemon juice and half the chopped parsley.

Drain the aubergines and squeeze dry using absorbent kitchen paper. Heat a little more olive oil, add the aubergines and lightly brown on either side. Place them side by side in a well-oiled oven dish. Spoon the tomato and onion filling into the slits of the aubergines and pour any surplus over them. Mix a little more sugar and salt together with the hot water and any remaining olive oil. Pour this over the aubergines and bake in the preheated oven for 45 minutes or until the aubergines are tender.

Set aside to cool. Transfer to a serving plate and garnish with the remaining chopped parsley.

Zeytinyağlı Pırasa

Leeks, carrots and rice cooked with olive oil

This popular dish evokes feelings of the winter vegetable markets, a delicious and comforting combination of rice and vegetables. Leeks and carrots are native to Anatolia, and purple carrots, which can still be found, add a fantastic dynamic to this dish. As with all *zeytinyağlı* dishes it can be cooked ahead of time and served cold as part of a main meal with wedges of lemon to squeeze over.

Serves 6
Preparation time - 15 minutes
Cooking time - 35 minutes

1/2 cup olive oil	2 cups hot water
1 medium onion, finely chopped	juice of 1 lemon
2 carrots, peeled and thinly sliced	1 teaspoon salt
1kg/2.2lbs fresh leeks	1 teaspoon sugar
washed and sliced diagonally into bite size pieces	chopped fresh dill for garnish
2 tablespoons of long grain rice, washed and drained	lemon wedges to squeeze over

In a large pan, gently heat the olive oil and sauté the onions and carrots for 5 minutes. Add the leeks and stir occasionally, taking care they do not scorch. When the vegetables are starting to soften and become bright in colour, add the rice, hot water, lemon juice, salt and sugar.

Cover and cook gently for 20 minutes or until the rice and vegetables are tender and the cooking liquid is absorbed. If necessary, add a little more hot water during cooking and avoid stirring, as this will disturb starch in the grains of rice.

Remove from the heat, cover with an absorbent kitchen cloth or paper and replace the lid in order to absorb any excess moisture. Set aside to cool.

Transfer to a serving dish, sprinkle with chopped dill and serve with lemon wedges to squeeze over.

Zeytinyağlı Kereviz

Celeriac baskets of winter vegetables with a lemon sauce

Celeriac is a knobbly root closely related to celery, and has an interesting flavour, a mix of aniseed, celery and parsley. The clever presentation of this dish requires the celeriac to be halved and each half slightly hollowed out to create a little basket. It is then served with the other vegetables perched on top.

Serves 4
Preparation time - 25 minutes
Cooking time - 30 minutes

4 small celeriacs, peeled	**2 cups hot water**
2 tablespoons peas, fresh or frozen	**salt and sugar to taste**
1 carrot, peeled and diced	**1 tablespoon plain white flour**
1 potato, peeled and diced	**juice of 1 lemon**
8 small shallots, peeled	**fresh dill for garnish**
1/2 cup olive oil	

To prevent discolouration during the preparation, keep the raw celeriac in a bowl of water with a squeeze of lemon juice. Cut each one in half horizontally and on the cut surface cut away a slight hollow. This hollow should be deep enough to accommodate the other vegetables when cooked.

If using fresh peas, cook separately until tender and put to one side.

Drain the celeriac and place in a pan together with the other prepared vegetables, olive oil, hot water and a little sugar and salt. Cook on a medium heat for about 20 minutes or until the vegetables are tender. Add the cooked peas and a little chopped dill, heat through and then remove from the heat.

Combine the lemon juice with the flour and a little water, add this to the pan and stir gently. Cook for a further 2 minutes, allowing the sauce to thicken a little. Remove from the heat and set aside to cool in the pan.

To serve, transfer the celeriac halves to a serving plate and distribute the other vegetables evenly on top. Pour the lemon sauce over and garnish with sprigs of dill.

Zeytinyağlı Dolma İçi

Aromatic rice for stuffing vegetables

Turkish people are very fond of stuffed vegetables - *dolma*. Stuffed tomatoes, peppers and aubergines are the year round favourites, cabbage leaves are stuffed in the winter months and vine leaves and courgette flowers herald a fresh option in springtime. The success of any great *dolma*, which literally means 'stuffed', relies heavily on getting the stuffing right and the generous use of onions is of utmost importance. This recipe is for the stuffing used in the *zeytinyağlı dolma* recipes, which are made without meat, and eaten cold as an entrée or meze. This recipe makes enough to stuff approximately 10-15 vegetables.

Serves 4 - 6
Preparation time - 15 minutes
Cooking time - 15 minutes

2 tablespoons currants
1 cup long grain rice
1/4 cup olive oil
2 tablespoons pine nuts
6 medium onions, finely chopped
1/2 teaspoon ground cinnamon

1/2 teaspoon ground allspice
1 cup hot water
salt and sugar to taste
freshly ground black pepper
1 cup fresh chopped herbs - mint, parsley and dill

Put the currants in hot water to allow them to swell; drain and put to one side. Soak the rice in hot salted water for 30 minutes. Rinse under cold running water and drain.

Heat the oil in a deep pan and gently sauté the pine nuts until golden. Add the chopped onion and sauté until soft. Add the drained rice, currants and spices, stirring gently to ensure the rice grains are evenly coated. Add the hot water, salt and sugar, stir once and continue cooking for about 10 minutes or until the cooking liquid is absorbed and steam holes appear in the surface of the rice. It is important not to stir the rice during this time.

Remove from the heat, cover the top of the pan with a cloth, replace the lid and set aside to cool for 20 minutes.

Season with freshly ground black pepper. Add the herbs and combine gently with a wooden spoon. The rice stuffing is now ready to stuff into vegetables of your choice.

Zeytinyağlı Biber ve Domates Dolması

Aromatic rice stuffed peppers and tomatoes cooked with olive oil

Serves 6
Preparation time - 15 minutes
Cooking time - 40 minutes

6 small green bell peppers
6 medium tomatoes
2 tomatoes, skinned and chopped
1/4 cup of olive oil
1 cup of hot water
salt and sugar to taste
aromatic rice stuffing for vegetables (page 43)
chopped parsley for garnish

Carefully cut a thin slice from the stem end of the peppers and tomatoes, reserving these pieces to use later. Remove the seeds and membranes, wash and drain.

Fill the peppers and tomatoes with the rice stuffing. Put the chopped tomatoes in a well-oiled, deep baking pan and place the stuffed vegetables on top as tightly packed as possible so they stay upright. Replace the lids. Whisk together the olive oil, hot water, sugar and salt and pour over.

Cover and bake in a moderate oven for about 40 minutes or until tender.

Set aside to cool and serve sprinkled with chopped parsley.

Zeytinyağlı Lahana ve Asma Yaprak Dolması

Cabbage and grapevine leaves stuffed with aromatic rice and cooked with olive oil

Cabbage *dolma* appear in winter. Spring heralds the fresh green leaves of the grape vine. Have a go at making these fantastic *dolma*, it is really not as hard as you would imagine and will certainly impress your guests.

Serves 6
Preparation time - 35 minutes
Cooking time - 30 minutes

**1 medium white cabbage/25 grapevine leaves
aromatic rice stuffing (page 43)
2 tablespoons olive oil
1 cup hot water
juice of 1/2 lemon
salt and sugar to taste
1 lemon, thinly sliced
sprigs of dill for garnish
lemon wedges to serve**

Cut the cabbage in half vertically and cut out the hearts. Plunge into a pot of boiling, salted water and cook for 5 minutes. The leaves should be tender but not over cooked. Rinse under cold running water and carefully remove the cuter leaves. Cut away the hard central vein, resulting in 25 pieces of cabbage the size of your hand.

One by one, place a walnut sized piece of rice stuffing at the base of each leaf, fold the edges inwards over the stuffing and roll up to form a finger sized dolma.

Line a large pan with any discarded cabbage leaves. Arrange the dolma in the pan seam side down and side by side, creating layers. Whisk together the water, olive oil, lemon juice, sugar and salt and pour over the dolma. Arrange the lemon slices on the top. Wet a circle of greaseproof paper lightly and place over the dolma. Place a dinner plate on top of this, which fits easily into the pan and acts as a weight.

Cover and cook over a low heat for about 30 minutes, or until the dolma are tender. Remove from the heat and set aside to cool. Transfer to a serving plate, drizzle with a little olive oil and garnish elegantly with sprigs of dill. Serve with lemon wedges to squeeze over.

Note - Alternatively for grapevine leaf dolma – Soften fresh leaves in boiling salted water, drain and rinse under cold running water. If using the preserved variety soak thoroughly in a few changes of water to remove the brine. Cut away the stalk and proceed as above.

Ekşili Patlıcan

Sweet and sour aubergine

Serves 4 - 6
Preparation time - 15 minutes
Cook time - 30 minutes

4 aubergines
2 onions, thinly sliced
3 tomatoes, peeled and chopped
6 cloves garlic, crushed in salt
1/2 cup olive oil
juice of 1 lemon
1 teaspoon salt
1 teaspoon sugar
chopped parsley for garnish

Remove the stem and peel the aubergines in alternate vertical stripes. Cut into bite-size chunks and place in a bowl of cold salted water for 30 minutes.

Drain the aubergines and squeeze dry in a towel. Place in a pan with the other ingredients. Cover and cook over a low heat until the aubergines are tender, most of the liquid has been absorbed and the sauce is rich.

Set aside to cool and serve garnished with a sprinkling of chopped parsley.

Kabak Mücveri

Courgette fritters flavoured with dill

Courgettes, also known as zucchini, are the most widely available summer squash in Turkey. They are very versatile, used in many dishes and their flowers are perfect for stuffing. Either as a meze or light lunch dish, these scrumptious little fritters are fantastic accompanied with garlic infused yogurt.

Serves 4 - 6
Preparation time - 15 minutes
Cooking time - 15 minutes

4 medium courgettes, grated
150g/6oz Turkish white cheese/feta
1 onion, finely chopped or
6 spring onions, finely chopped
1 tablespoon chopped dill
5 tablespoons plain white flour

1/2 teaspoon baking soda
2 eggs, beaten
pinch of paprika (optional)
salt and pepper to taste
sunflower oil for frying
sprigs of dill for garnish

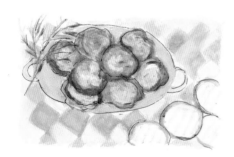

Place the grated courgette in a colander, sprinkle with a little salt and leave to drain for 30 minutes. Crumble or grate the white cheese.

Squeeze out any excess water from the courgettes and put in a bowl.

Add the remaining ingredients, season with salt and pepper and beat into a batter. (Take care not to add salt if your cheese is salty). Leave to stand for 30 minutes.

In a frying pan heat enough sunflower oil to shallow fry. Using a tablespoon, drop into the hot oil spoonfuls of the batter mix. Fry on both sides until golden brown, remove with a straining spoon and drain on absorbent kitchen paper.

Serve hot and crispy from the pan or make in advance to be enjoyed cold as a meze. Garnish with sprigs of dill and accompany with garlic infused yogurt.

Note - Summer squash is an effective diuretic and its potassium content benefits those with high blood pressure. Dill is known to aid digestion.

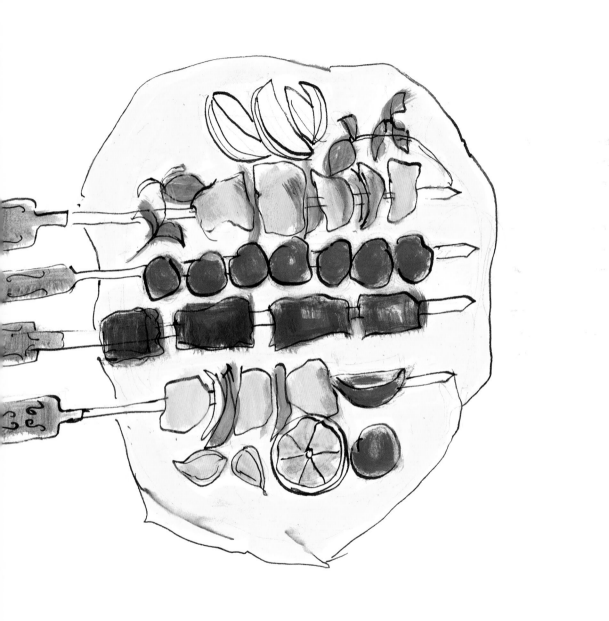

Et ve Tavuk Yemekleri

Meat and Chicken Dishes

During their early days of migration from central Asia, the nomadic Turks relied on their horses and herds for their day-to-day existence. They travelled the steppes westward in search of grazing for their livestock, hunting game and supplementing their diet with wild berries and vegetation growing along the way. Milk from their sheep and goats was preserved to provide yogurt and cheese, and *kımız,* a drink made from fermented mare's milk was the tipple with a kick, that ensured celebrations went with a bang. Meat would be cooked on the evening campfire using makeshift skewers – *kebabs*. When wood was scarce or in order not to alert others of their presence, meat was chopped finely and pounded with spices and herbs and eaten raw – *çiğ köfte*. When plentiful, meat was preserved and placed under the saddles of the warriors' horses to be tenderized in sweat and then hung in the dry winds to cure. Present day *pastırma*, a cured fillet of beef coated in a combination of spices, has its origins in these early times.

The early rulers of the Ottoman Empire also pursued a passion for hunting; the forests of Bolu became a particular favourite. The chefs of this area became renowned for their imaginative cooking skills and their inventive recipes are considered the cornerstone of many Turkish dishes enjoyed today. Bolu still has a reputation for being the breeding ground for Turkey's greatest chefs.

Hünkar Beğendi

Sultan's delight - lamb ragout on a bed of puréed aubergine

This classic lamb dish is served on a bed of smoky tasting aubergine combined with cheese in a béchamel sauce. Empress Eugenie, the wife of Napoleon III, particularly admired the purée and ordered her chef to learn the technique during a visit to the Topkapı Palace. Once you've mastered the aubergine purée, it goes well with any grilled meat and chicken. Try it with spicy meatballs and topped with a garlicky tomato sauce.

Serves 4
Preparation time - 40 minutes
Cooking time - 1 hour

For the lamb ragout -	*For the aubergine purée -*
500g/1.1lbs cubed leg of lamb	**6 large/1kg/2lbs aubergines**
1 medium onion, finely chopped	**squeeze of lemon juice**
2 tablespoons butter	**4 tablespoons butter**
1 small green bell pepper, seeded and chopped	**3 tablespoons plain white flour**
2 garlic cloves, crushed	**1 1/2 cups warm milk**
2 tomatoes, skinned and chopped	**1/2 cup hard mature cheese, grated**
1 1/2 cups hot water	**salt and freshly ground black pepper**
2 tablespoons tomato paste	**grated nutmeg**
salt and freshly ground black pepper	
chopped parsley for garnish	

Sauté the chopped onions gently in the butter until soft. Season the meat with the salt and pepper and add to the onions, stirring occasionally until evenly browned. Add the chopped green pepper and garlic and when these are sizzling add the chopped tomatoes and continue cooking until the juice has evaporated. Add the hot water and the tomato paste, cover and simmer for about 1 hour or until the meat is tender. Take care it doesn't dry out and add a little more water if necessary. Check the seasoning and adjust accordingly.

Cook the aubergines on a barbecue grill or over an open gas flame, turning occasionally by the stalks until the outer skin is charred and blistered and the inner flesh soft. Alternatively, they can be baked in a hot oven. Peel away the burnt skin and discard the stalks. Put the flesh in a colander to drain away any bitter juices and then mash together with the lemon juice, using a fork or potato masher.

Melt the butter on a low heat. Add the flour and beat well to make a roux. Slowly add the warm milk, whisking thoroughly to get a smooth consistency, and cook for 5 minutes. Add the mashed aubergine, a little salt and freshly ground black pepper, and simmer gently for a further 5 minutes. Remove from the heat, stir in the cheese and a little freshly grated nutmeg and simmer gently for a further 2 minutes.

Serve hot, the meat sitting on top of a bed of the aubergine purée, and garnish generously with chopped parsley.

Note – If you reheat the purée you may need to add a little more milk to ensure you achieve the correct consistency.

Kadınbudu Köfte

Lady's thigh köfte – spicy meat rissoles in a crispy coating

Visions of the Sultan and his harem, how else could this name have originated? Of all the saucy names given during the days of old, this has to be one of the most provocative. Actually nothing like thighs, they are great served for a picnic lunch and are easily prepared in advance to quickly rustle up for a tasty supper.

Serves 4 - 6
Preparation time - 30 minutes
Cooking time - 15 minutes

1/2 cup/100g rice
450g/1lb lean minced beef
1 tablespoon butter
1 medium onion, grated
1/4 cup of parsley, finely chopped
1/2 teaspoon ground cinnamon
1/2 teaspoon ground allspice

1/2 teaspoon ground cumin
1/2 teaspoon ground black pepper
1 teaspoon salt
3 tablespoons plain flour for dipping
3 eggs, 2 beaten for dipping
sunflower oil for frying

Rinse the rice and add to a pan of boiling water. Cook for 15 minutes or until tender, drain, rinse under cold water and set aside.

Sauté half the meat in the butter and cook until any moisture is absorbed. Remove from the heat and set aside.

In a large bowl, put the remaining meat together with the cooked rice, onion, parsley, spices, salt and pepper and one egg. Add the cooked meat and knead well into a paste. Refrigerate until required.

With wet hands, take large egg sized portions and roll into balls and then flatten into oval shapes. The mixture should make about 12 köfte. Dip them into the flour and then beaten egg. Shallow fry in hot oil until brown on both sides. Drain on absorbent kitchen paper.

Serve hot with a fresh salad or cold as part of a picnic lunch.

Note - Keeping your hands wet when making any type of köfte prevents the mixture sticking to your hands and makes the process so much more manageable.

Karnıyarık

Split belly aubergines stuffed with ground beef, onions and tomatoes

This dish is a legacy of the palace kitchens and yet another of the imperial demands for ingenuity concerning the much loved aubergine. You will find this dish wherever you go in Turkey.

Serves 6
Preparation time - 30 minutes
Cooking time - 45 minutes

6 aubergines (long thin variety)
225g/1/2lb minced lean beef or lamb
1 large onion, finely chopped
6 garlic cloves, finely chopped
3 tomatoes, skinned and chopped
1 tablespoon tomato paste
1/2 cup olive oil

sugar to taste
salt and freshly ground black pepper
1/2 cup parsley, chopped
6 slices of tomato - for decorative topping
3 sweet green peppers, seeded - for decorative topping

Preheat oven to 180c/350f/gas mark 4.

With a sharp peeler, partially peel the aubergines in alternate vertical stripes from stem to base, leaving the stalk intact. In each aubergine cut a deep slit lengthways without cutting through to the skin on the opposite side and leaving 1.5cm/1/2 in uncut at either end. Place the peeled aubergines in a bowl of salted water placing a plate on top to hold them beneath the surface.

In a little of the olive oil, sauté the onions until soft. Add the minced meat and cook until any moisture is absorbed. Add the garlic, tomatoes, tomato paste and sugar to taste. Season with salt and freshly ground black pepper. Continue cooking for a further 5 minutes. Remove from the heat and stir in most of the chopped parsley, reserving some for the final garnish.

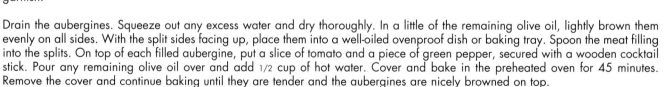

Drain the aubergines. Squeeze out any excess water and dry thoroughly. In a little of the remaining olive oil, lightly brown them evenly on all sides. With the split sides facing up, place them into a well-oiled ovenproof dish or baking tray. Spoon the meat filling into the splits. On top of each filled aubergine, put a slice of tomato and a piece of green pepper, secured with a wooden cocktail stick. Pour any remaining olive oil over and add 1/2 cup of hot water. Cover and bake in the preheated oven for 45 minutes. Remove the cover and continue baking until they are tender and the aubergines are nicely browned on top.

Serve hot, garnished with the remaining parsley.

Note - Peeling the aubergines and soaking them in salted water helps to remove any bitter juices and prevents them from soaking up too much oil in the cooking process. However, there is evidence that aubergines available today are not bitter and therefore some cooks choose not to bother.

İçli Köfte

Mother in law's crispy coated meat and nut rissoles

Though this is not a literal translation, this type of *köfte* signifies a tradition still practised in Anatolia. Before a wedding, the groom's mother makes these *köfte* for her future daughter-in-law to signify that her lips are now sealed with discretion. The lamb for the filling should be slightly fatty to ensure it stays moist during cooking, and it is also preferable to have the meat minced twice for the best result. The köfte can be served on a bed of salad leaves as an entrée, or as part of a main course.

Serves 4 - 6
Preparation time - 30 minutes
Cooking time - 40 minutes

For the filling -
250g/8oz minced lamb or beef
1 tablespoon butter
1 medium onion, finely chopped
4 garlic cloves, crushed
1/2 cup walnuts, crushed
1/2 cup blanched pistachio nuts, crushed
1/2 teaspoon ground cumin
1/2 teaspoon ground allspice
1/2 teaspoon ground paprika
salt and freshly ground black pepper
handful of chopped parsley

For the crispy coating -
250g/8oz minced beef
1 1/4 cups fine bulgur wheat, rinsed and drained
1 teaspoon paprika flakes
salt and freshly ground black pepper
1 egg, beaten
plain white flour for dipping
sunflower oil for deep frying

To make the filling, heat the butter and sauté the onions until soft, add the meat, garlic, nuts and spices, season with salt and black pepper and cook for a further 10 minutes. Add the chopped parsley and set aside to cool.

To make the crispy coating, put the bulgur and paprika flakes together in a bowl, season with salt and black pepper and add 1/2 cup of warm water. Knead well until the bulgur softens and the grains are sticking together. If the mixture is too dry and crumbly, wet your hands and work some more. Add the meat for the coating and the beaten egg and work for 10-15 minutes into the consistency of dough.

With wet hands take a piece of the crispy coating mix, the size of an egg, roll it into a ball, push a hole into it with your forefinger to create a hollow. Try to make the sides as thin as possible without it crumbling, spoon in some filling and close up the hole. Taper the ends to a point resembling a lemon and continue until all the mixture is used up. As you make them, keep covered with a damp cloth to prevent them drying out.

Heat some sunflower oil and deep-fry the köfte until golden brown and the outer coatings are crunchy. Be careful not to put too many in the pan at one time. Drain on absorbent kitchen paper.

Serve hot or cold with a salad accompaniment.

Note - Bulgur wheat is available in fine and coarse grains. The fine type is generally used for köfte and the coarser one for pilaf.

Arnavut Ciğeri

Albanian spiced liver on a bed of red onion

Throughout all the regions once dominated by the Ottoman Empire you will find liver cooked in this way. The dish relies on the tenderest veal or lamb's liver so often found in Turkey. The liver is cubed, cooked in spices and served usually as a meze on a bed of red onion combined with chopped parsley and sumac, the crushed dried berry of the sumac tree which imparts a tangy citrus taste. Spear each piece with a cocktail stick as a good option for a drinks party.

Serves 4 - 6
Preparation time - 20 minutes
Cooking time - 5 minutes

450g/1lb lamb's liver, cut into cubes	freshly ground black pepper
2 tablespoons plain white flour	4 garlic cloves, finely chopped
1 teaspoon paprika flakes	1 teaspoon ground sumac
1 teaspoon ground cumin	1 red onion, thinly sliced
1 teaspoon dried thyme	1/2 cup of chopped parsley
1 teaspoon salt	sunflower oil for frying

In a bowl combine the flour, paprika, cumin, thyme, salt and some freshly ground black pepper. Add the cubes of liver and toss well, making sure it is evenly coated. Shake in a sieve to remove any excess flour.

In a frying pan, heat the oil and sauté the garlic for about 30 seconds. Add the liver and cook on a high heat turning constantly to ensure it is evenly cooked. It is important the liver is crispy on the outside but not overcooked. Add 1/2 the chopped parsley and remove from the heat.

Serve on a bed of sliced red onion tossed with the remaining parsley and ground sumac.

Terbiyeli Köfte

Well behaved köfte in a tangy egg and lemon sauce

This dish dates back to the times of culinary experimentation in the Ottoman palace kitchens and literally translates as 'well behaved meatballs'. It can be served as a main course or alternatively as soup, which requires making the meatballs very small. Either way it is served with lots of sauce, so make sure you have lots of freshly baked bread to go with it. The terbiye sauce is added just before serving, as it can curdle if overheated or reheated.

Serves 4 - 6
Preparation time - 30 minutes
Cooking time - 35 minutes

For the meatballs -
450g/1lb minced lamb or beef
1 tablespoon rice, rinsed and drained
1 small onion, grated
1 handful of finely chopped parsley
1 handful finely chopped dill
1 teaspoon salt
freshly ground black pepper
2 tablespoons plain white flour

For the stock -
2 potatoes, peeled and diced
2 carrots, peeled and diced
1 small celeriac, peeled and diced
(tender stalks and leaves may also be used)
2 teaspoons salt
4 cups/1 litre boiling water

For the terbiye sauce -
2 egg yolks
pinch of salt
juice of 1 lemon
chopped parsley or dill for garnish

Place the prepared vegetables in water with a squeeze of lemon to prevent discolouration.

Combine the minced meat, rice, grated onion, (keeping any residual onion juice to add to the stock) parsley, dill, salt and freshly ground black pepper. Knead well to form a paste. With wet hands roll into balls the size of walnuts and then roll in flour. This makes about 20. Put them in the fridge whilst preparing the stock.

In a large pan heat the water with the salt. When it is boiling, drain the vegetables and add to the pan. Once the vegetables are simmering add the meatballs. Continue to simmer for 15 minutes until the rice grains are protruding from the meatballs and the vegetables tender. Remove from the heat.

Put the egg yolks into a bowl. Add the pinch of salt and whisk with a fork. Add the lemon juice and continue whisking, adding spoonfuls of the hot stock a little at a time. Return this mixture to the pan and on a gentle heat continue stirring until the sauce thickens. Take care not to allow it to reach a rapid boil.

Serve at once, garnished with fresh parsley and dill and accompanied with a rice pilaf.

Etli Kabak Dolması

Courgettes stuffed with meat, rice and herbs in a tomato sauce.

This meaty rice stuffing mixture can also be used to stuff aubergines, peppers, cabbage leaves, grapevine leaves and courgette flowers. It is sufficient to stuff approximately 10 vegetables or 25 leaves, depending on their size. Courgettes are used in this dish, their centres hollowed out and stuffed and then baked in a tomato sauce. Try to use fat courgettes, which will be easier to hollow out, and if necessary cut them in half to avoid splitting them. Meat dolmas are served hot and accompanied with tomato sauce or garlicky yogurt; they make an extremely good lunch option.

Serves 4 - 6
Preparation time - 20 minutes
Cooking time - 40 minutes

For the stuffing -
1/4 cup of rice, soaked in hot water for 30 minutes
450g/1lb minced lamb or beef
1 onion, grated
1/2 cup of finely chopped parsley, mint and dill
2 tomatoes, peeled and chopped
2 tablespoons tomato paste
salt and freshly ground black pepper

10 courgettes
3 tablespoons butter
3 tomatoes, peeled and finely chopped
salt and sugar to taste
2 tablespoons tomato paste
2 cups water
chopped dill for garnish

For the stuffing, rinse the rice under cold running water and drain. Place all the ingredients for the stuffing in a bowl and mix well, kneading with your hands to create a well-combined paste.

Cut off the ends of the courgettes. Score the outer skins with a fork lengthways evenly to create striped indentations. With a corer, scoop out the inner seeds, leaving a shell of about 1cm/1/2 in in diameter, creating a hollow for the meat stuffing. If necessary cut the courgettes in half to achieve this and to avoid splitting the sides.

Loosely fill the courgette shells with the prepared rice and meat stuffing using the end of a wooden spoon to poke it in. Place them in a well-oiled oven proof dish alongside one another.

Melt the butter and add the chopped tomatoes, a little sugar and salt. Cook gently until it thickens slightly. Stir in the tomato paste and water and pour over the courgettes.

Cover and bake in a moderate oven for about 1 hour or until the courgettes are tender and the rice filling cooked.

Serve hot with the tomato sauce drizzled over and a sprinkling of chopped dill for garnish.

Note – To make garlic yogurt, crush 2 cloves of garlic with a pinch of salt in a pestle and mortar and whisk into 2 cups of creamy natural yogurt.

Cızbız Köfte

Sizzling grilled meatballs

These meatballs get their name from the sizzling sound they make as the melting fat drips from the meat on to the hot embers of the barbecue grill. Make sure the embers of the grill are hot and brush the grill generously with oil before cooking.

Serves 4 - 6
Preparation time - 20 minutes
Cooking time - 10 minutes

2 slices of stale bread,
(soaked in water and squeezed dry)
450g/1lb minced beef or lamb
1 medium onion, grated
2 garlic cloves, crushed with salt

1 teaspoon ground cumin
2 teaspoon salt
freshly ground black pepper
1 teaspoon bicarbonate of soda
parsley to garnish

Discard the crusts of the bread and crumble the rest into a bowl. Add all the other ingredients and knead well until the mixture resembles a soft dough.

With wet hands take a piece the size of a walnut, roll into a ball and then slightly flatten. Continue until all the mixture is used. Cover and store in the fridge until required.

Grill until brown on both sides. Serve garnished with parsley.

Tavuk Şiş Kebabı

Succulent chicken shish kebab

Şiş (shish) – is quite simply the word in Turkish for skewer. Cooking meat over the open campfire on makeshift skewers dates back to the time Turkic tribes migrated from Central Asia in the 6th century. A shish kebab can be made with chicken, lamb or veal, and is often combined on the skewer with onions, tomatoes and peppers.

Serves 4 - 6
Preparation time - 10 minutes
Cooking time - 10 minutes

1kg/2lbs boned chicken, cut into cubes
2 garlic cloves, crushed with salt
1 onion, grated
6 tablespoons natural yogurt

6 tablespoons olive oil
1 teaspoon dried thyme/oregano
freshly ground black pepper to taste

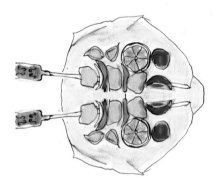

In a bowl, mix together all the ingredients except the chicken. Dry the chicken well on absorbent kitchen paper and add to the marinade. Cover and leave for 1 hour or overnight in the refrigerator.

Thread the chicken pieces tightly on skewers.

Grill until brown on both sides, brushing generously with the marinade as they cook.

Serve hot with salad and pilaf.

Note – Yogurt, when used as part of a marinade, assists the break down of enzymes and helps tenderise the meat.

İzmir Köfte

Casserole of meatballs, potatoes, tomatoes and peppers

An Aegean favourite, this casserole can either be cooked on the stovetop or baked in the oven. It makes a hearty main course served with plain white rice, salad and a bowl of *cacık* (page 21).

Serves 4 - 6
Preparation time - 30 minutes
Cooking time - 30 minutes

For the köfte -
450g/1lb minced beef or lamb
1 medium onion, grated
3 slices of stale bread, soaked in water and squeezed dry
1 egg, beaten
1 teaspoon dried mint
1 teaspoon ground cumin
1 cup of finely chopped parsley
1 teaspoon salt
freshly ground black pepper
1/2 cup plain white flour
sunflower oil for frying

And the rest -
6 potatoes, sliced
1 green bell pepper, deseeded and sliced
3 tomatoes, sliced
2 tablespoons tomato paste
2 tablespoons butter

Discard the crusts of the bread and crumble the rest into a bowl. Add all the köfte ingredients except the flour and oil and only half of the chopped parsley. Knead well until the mixture resembles a soft dough. With wet hands take a piece the size of a large walnut and roll into a large finger shape about 2.5cm/1in. thick. Continue until all the mixture is used. The meatballs can now be covered and stored in the fridge until required.

Lightly fry the potato slices until they start to go translucent and golden. Drain on absorbent kitchen paper.

Roll the prepared meatballs in the flour. Heat a little oil in a frying pan and fry them on both sides until crisp and lightly browned. Drain on absorbent kitchen paper.

Using some of the butter, grease an oven dish. Create layers with the potatoes, meatballs and sliced tomatoes. Top with the sliced green pepper and season with salt and freshly ground black pepper.

Dilute the tomato paste in a cup of hot water and pour over the top. Dot the top with the remaining butter, cover and bake in a moderate oven for 30 minutes or until the potatoes are soft and the sauce has thickened.

Serve hot, garnished with the remaining parsley.

Terbiyeli Kuzu Kapama

Slow cooked lamb and spring greens with a lemon and egg sauce

This is a celebration of springtime, everything fresh from the garden with tender young lamb to melt in the mouth!

Serves 6
Preparation time - 10 minutes
Cooking time – 1 1/2 hours

6 shins of spring lamb
12 spring onions, roughly chopped
6 garlic cloves, sliced
1 lettuce
Swiss chard or spring greens, tough stalks removed
4 tablespoons butter
salt and freshly ground black pepper
sugar to taste
1/2 cup fresh dill, chopped

For the lemon and egg sauce (terbiye) -
2 egg yolks
juice of 1/2 lemon
2 tablespoons plain white flour

Put the lamb in a pan and cover with water. Bring to the boil and cook for 30 minutes.

Drain the lamb, reserving 1 cup of the cooking fluid and rinse under cold running water. Return to the pan and season with salt and black pepper. Sprinkle a little sugar over, add the spring onions, as much garlic as you wish and cover with torn lettuce and chard leaves. Dot the top with butter, season again with salt and black pepper and sprinkle with half the dill. Add the cup of cooking fluid, cover and cook on a very low heat for 45-60 minutes or until the lamb is falling away from the bones.

If desired, the resulting stock can be used to create an egg and lemon sauce. Beat together egg yolks, lemon juice and flour. Add a little of the hot stock to this mixture a spoonful at a time. Return to the pan and heat thoroughly, taking care not to let it boil. Serve over the lamb and vegetables.

Serve with pilaf, garnished with the remaining dill.

Çiğ Köfte

Spicy tartare meatballs

These meatballs do not require any cooking and are often said to contain up to 30 different spices. They are considered a delicacy in southeastern Turkey. Traditionally, they are made with lamb but beef will do; the real trick is to really pound the mix well so that the meat is almost undetectable. It is traditionally a dish made by men, who share the work of kneading the mixture for 20 minutes. It is a test of strength and masculinity. With the right combination of spices these *köfte* are truly delicious. Have the meat minced twice.

Serves 4 - 6
Preparation time - 45 minutes

250g/10 oz lean lamb or beef (well minced)
1 cup fine bulgur wheat
1 onion, grated
3 spring onions, finely chopped
6 garlic cloves, crushed with salt
2 tablespoons tomato paste
1 teaspoon paprika paste
1 teaspoon salt
1 teaspoon paprika
1/2 teaspoon paprika flakes

2 teaspoons ground cumin
1/2 teaspoon ground coriander
1/2 teaspoon allspice
1/2 teaspoon ground cinnamon
1/4 teaspoon ground cloves
freshly ground black pepper
1/2 cup of parsley, finely chopped
lemon wedges to serve
lettuce leaves to serve
parsley for garnish

Soak the bulgur in 1 cup of hot water for 20 minutes. Drain and squeeze out any excess water. Place the bulgur in a bowl with the meat and knead well to a smooth consistency.

Add the chopped onions, garlic, tomato and paprika paste and knead well, followed by the salt, spices and parsley. Continue kneading for 20 minutes. Taking a spoonful at a time, with wet hands shape them into balls the size of large walnuts and with your finger create a small indentation. Refrigerate until required.

Serve on a generous bed of parsley and lettuce leaves and decorate with lemon wedges. To eat, squeeze lemon juice into the indentations and roll up in a crunchy lettuce leaf.

Note - Paprika has wide-ranging strengths, from sweet and piquant to dynamite hot. It is found in powdered form (kırmızı biber) and crushed flakes (pul biber), rubbed in oil to preserve taste and freshness. Pastes are also available and can be firey, so use with caution!

Çerkez Tavuğu

Circassian chicken with walnuts

During the Ottoman reign, the Sultans took a particular liking to women of Circassian origin and many were captured to serve in the harems as concubines and wives. These fair beauties delighted the Sultans and with them came this dish. Originally the dish was made with fresh coriander leaves, used liberally in Circassian cuisine. However, the palace chefs decided to create their own tamer version. This is a great option for a light lunch, served with a green salad and toast.

Serves 6 - 8
Preparation time - 30 minutes
Cooking time - 1 hour

For the chicken stock -
1 whole medium sized chicken
1 onion, quartered
1 carrot, peeled and sliced
4 cloves
4 allspice berries
4 bay leaves
1 teaspoon coriander seeds
salt and black pepper to taste

For the walnut dressing -
3 slices stale bread, crusts removed
3 1/2 cups/350g walnuts, ground
6 garlic cloves, crushed with salt
1 teaspoon paprika
salt and black pepper to taste
1/2 cup of coriander leaves, chopped
(optional)

For the garnish -
1 tablespoon olive oil
1 teaspoon paprika
1 handful shelled walnuts
chopped parsley

Put the chicken, stock ingredients and enough water to almost cover the chicken in a large pan. Season with salt and pepper. Cover and simmer for about an hour or until the chicken is tender.

Remove the chicken from the pan and set aside to cool. Simmer the stock for a further 20 minutes. Strain through a colander and put the strained cooking liquid aside to cool. When the chicken is cool enough to handle, discard the skin, strip the meat from the bones, tear into thin strips and put to one side.

For the walnut dressing soak the bread in a little of the reserved cooking liquid. Squeeze dry and crumble the bread into a bowl with the ground walnuts, garlic and paprika. In a food processor, blitz these together to form a paste. Add a spoonful at a time of reserved cooking liquid until a creamy consistency is obtained. Fold in the coriander leaves, if using, and season with salt and pepper if required.

In a bowl combine the chicken pieces with half the walnut dressing. Pour onto a serving plate, cover with the remaining sauce, and refrigerate until required.

Heat the olive oil and add the paprika. Cook gently for 1 minute.

To serve, sprinkle the dressed chicken with chopped walnuts, sprigs of parsley and a drizzle of the paprika infused oil.

Adana Kebap

Charcoal grilled spicy lamb kebabs

Adana lies in the southeast of Turkey in a region known for its hot spicy food. Minced lamb is combined with spices and moulded in a long sausage shape on special long, flat bladed skewers. After being grilled over a charcoal fire, the kebab is eased off the skewer and served on top of warm strips of freshly baked pide bread, accompanied with tomatoes, peppers and a salad of sliced onions tossed in ground sumac and chopped parsley. Sumac is a crushed dried berry which grows in the Middle East and Italy and is known to have been used by the Romans to impart a fruity but tart flavour, long before lemons came onto the scene.

Makes 8 kebabs
Preparation time - 20 minutes
Cooking time - 15 minutes

1kg/2.2lbs minced lamb
2 onions, finely chopped or grated
2 chilli peppers, finely chopped
3 cloves garlic, crushed with salt
1/2 cup of parsley, finely chopped
1 teaspoon paprika
1 teaspoon ground sumac
salt and freshly ground black pepper

To serve -
pide bread
grilled tomatoes and sweet long green peppers
1 onion, thinly sliced and dressed
with ground sumac and chopped parsley

Mix together the ingredients for the kebab. Knead thoroughly until smooth and divide into 8 portions. Work each portion along a flat bladed skewer to form a long flat sausage shape. Alternatively make into hamburger shaped patties.

Grill on either side over a charcoal grill until well browned.

Grill the tomatoes and green peppers and serve with the kebabs as suggested above.

Bamyalı Piliç

Casserole of chicken cooked with okra

Okra didn't find its way to Turkey until the 17th century. The Ottomans embraced it and since then it has become a firm favourite at mealtimes during the summer months. It can often be seen threaded on twine and strung across balconies to dry in the hot sun for use in the wintertime.

Serves 4 - 6
Preparation time - 20 minutes
Cooking time - 1 hour

**1 whole chicken, cut into 8 portions
500g/1lb okra
4 tablespoons butter/margarine
1 onion, finely chopped
3 large tomatoes, roughly chopped
grated zest of 1 lemon
2 teaspoons dried thyme
juice of 2 lemons
salt and pepper to taste**

Pare away the stalk end of the okra to resemble a cone. Place in a bowl of cold water with the juice of 1 lemon and a little salt. Leave to soak for 30 minutes.

In a large pan, melt the butter and brown the chicken portions. Remove the chicken, add the chopped onions and sauté until soft. Return the chicken to the pan and add the chopped tomatoes and lemon zest. Season with salt and pepper and sprinkle with dried thyme.

Drain the okra and arrange over the top. Sprinkle over the remaining lemon juice, cover and cook on a low heat until the chicken and okra are tender. Add a little water during cooking time only if necessary.

Serve hot with steaming mashed potato or plain white rice.

Note - Once okra are cut, it is important to immerse in water with either lemon juice or vinegar. This protects their fresh colour and also prevents the gelatinous juices of the okra affecting the finished dish.

Papaz Yahnisi

Priest's beef and onion ragout

Named after a priest, the origin of this dish may be Greek. Lamb and beef are both suitable, though using beef creates a rich and delicious gravy.

Serves 6
Preparation time - 10 minutes
Cooking time - 2 1/2 hours

1kg/2lb lean cubed beef	**3 tablespoons wine vinegar**
4 tablespoons plain white flour	**2 tomatoes, diced**
salt and pepper to taste	**1 teaspoon sugar**
4 tablespoons butter/margarine	**1 teaspoon ground allspice**
500g/1lb peeled pearl onions or shallots	**1 teaspoon ground cinnamon**
10 garlic cloves	**chopped parsley for garnish**

Toss the cubed beef in seasoned flour. Melt the margarine and sauté the beef for 5 minutes. Add the pearl onions and whole cloves of garlic and sauté everything together for a further 5 minutes.

Add the vinegar, tomatoes, sugar and spices. Stir well and then add 2 cups of boiling water. Cover and cook slowly on a low heat for about 2 hours or until the meat is tender.

Serve hot with a white rice pilaf, garnished with chopped parsley.

Note – Garlic and onion are the two oldest remedies known to man. Both contain allicin, which stimulates the body's antioxidant mechanisms and helps to combat the formation of clogged arteries.

Kuzu Pirzola

Grilled lamb chops marinated in mountain herbs

There is nothing more delicious than a tender mouthful of lamb conveniently attached to a useful bone handle. Quite simply, these chops are combined in a herb marinade and then the bones are wrapped attractively in aluminium cooking foil. They are grilled briefly until just cooked and beautifully succulent. They can be cooked under a conventional grill or over barbecue coals.

Serves 4 - 6
Preparation time - 10 minutes
Cooking time - 10 minutes

8-12 trimmed lamb chops
2 cloves garlic, crushed with salt
small handful of fresh rosemary or
2 teaspoons dried rosemary
1 onion, grated
4 tablespoons olive oil
2 teaspoons dried oregano/thyme
freshly ground black pepper to taste

Crush the garlic in a pestle and mortar with a little salt. Add the rosemary and crush it to release its aromatic oil and flavour. Add this to the grated onion, olive oil and oregano. Season with freshly ground black pepper.

Marinate the chops in this mixture for at least an hour or overnight in the refrigerator.

Grill until brown on both sides, brushing generously with the marinade as they cook.

Serve hot with salad and pilaf.

Note - Rosemary has a reputation for invigorating the circulation, improving the respiratory system and even relieving headaches.

Kuzu ve Ayva Yahnisi

Casserole of lamb with quince and cinnamon

The early writings of the Islamic mystics, known today as the 'whirling dervishes', provide great insight into Turkish cuisine during its development. Food became of great importance to the Order, symbolising spiritual sustenance, and its preparation, purification of the soul. Lamb dishes cooked with apples, quinces and figs were recorded and these dishes still retain popularity in the more conservative cities of Konya and Bursa today.

Serves 4 - 6
Preparation time - 15 minutes
Cooking time - 1 hour

1kg/2.2lbs boned lamb, cut into large cubes
2 quinces
squeeze of lemon juice
3 tablespoons butter/oil
10 pearl onions/shallots, peeled
4 garlic cloves, crushed with salt
1 teaspoon ground cinnamon

1/2 teaspoon cloves
1 tablespoon tomato paste
1 cup hot water
salt and freshly ground black pepper to taste
1/2 cup of parsley, chopped
1 tablespoon honey

Preheat oven to 200c/400f/gas mark 6.

Peel the quinces, remove the cores and cut into 8 segments. Immediately put them in cold water with a squeeze of lemon juice to prevent discolouration.

In a large pan, heat the butter or oil. Brown the lamb, remove and put to one side.

Add the onions and garlic and cook for a few minutes until they start to soften. Stir in the spices and return the meat to the pan. Stir well to ensure the meat is well coated. Add the tomato paste and the water, season with salt and pepper and simmer for 30 minutes.

Stir in the parsley and then transfer to an ovenproof dish. Drain the quince, lay the segments on top and drizzle with honey.

Place in the preheated oven for 30 minutes and cook until the quince segments are nicely caramelised.

Serve hot from the oven with pilaf.

Kuru Köfte

Crispy picnic meatballs

Although the name in Turkish implies that these meatballs are dry, nothing could be further from the truth, it just means to say they are served without a sauce. Generally pan-fried, these tasty mouthfuls can be served hot from the pan with pilaf or precooked to serve as finger food at a drinks party. Once cooked they are easy to pack and transport, and are commonly associated with travelling and picnics.

Serves 4 - 6
Preparation time - 20 minutes
Cooking time - 15 minutes

450g/1lb minced beef or lamb
1 medium onion, grated
3 slices of stale bread, soaked in water and squeezed dry
1 egg, beaten
1 teaspoon dried thyme or oregano

1/2 cup of parsley, finely chopped
1 teaspoon salt
freshly ground black pepper
1/2 cup plain white flour
sunflower oil for frying

Discard the crusts of the bread and crumble the rest into a bowl. Add all the ingredients except the flour and oil and only half the chopped parsley. Knead well with your hands, making sure everything is well combined, until the mixture resembles a soft dough.

With wet hands take a piece the size of a large walnut, roll into a large finger shape about 2.5cm/1in thick. Continue until all the mixture is used. They can now be covered and stored in the fridge until required.

Before frying, roll the meatballs in the flour. Heat 2.5cm/1in of oil in a frying pan over a medium to high heat and fry the meatballs on both sides till crisp and lightly browned.

Serve garnished with the remaining chopped parsley.

Serve hot or cold with a salad accompaniment.

Deniz Ürünleri

Fish and Seafood

Turkey's shores are host to varying and interesting waters: the Mediterranean and Aegean dominate the south and west, whilst the Dardanelles feed the Marmara sea which in turn filters through Istanbul's Bosphorus, culminating in the Black Sea to the north.

Each region enjoys local specialities; bluefish (*lüfer*) is a popular favourite in Istanbul and the Black Sea anchovy (*hamsi*) is a key ingredient in scores of dishes. Historically, only coastal inhabitants ate fish; the Turks who migrated from Central Asia were slow to absorb this new addition to their culinary culture. Nor did the Ottomans choose to lavish themselves with the fruits of the sea until the 19th century when the French influence of that period contradicted the common belief that the fish may come alive inside them when they drank a glass of water.

Today, however, fish and seafood are highly regarded and although invariably fish is served whole, grilled or fried there are plenty of inspired and delicious dishes to be found.

Kılıç Şiş

Grilled swordfish on skewers

Any firm-fleshed fish can be substituted, if swordfish is out of season or difficult to find. As with most fish dishes, freshness of produce is most important in order to obtain the most succulent and tasty result.

Serves 6
Preparation time - 20 minutes
Cooking time - 10 minutes

For the shish -
1kg/2.2lb boned swordfish
2 lemons, cut into 1/2 moon slices
2 tomatoes, cut into 1/2 moon slices
2 sweet green peppers
(cut in chunks)
rocket leaves for garnish

For the marinade -
2 tablespoons lemon juice
2 tablespoons olive oil
1 grated onion
2 teaspoons salt
1 1/2 teaspoons paprika
12 bay leaves

For the dressing -
juice of 1 lemon
1/2 cup olive oil
salt to taste
parsley, finely chopped

Cut the swordfish into matchbox size pieces. Combine the ingredients for the marinade, add the swordfish and refrigerate for 4-6 hours. Whisk together the ingredients for the dressing.

Thread the swordfish on to well-oiled skewers at intervals with pieces of lemon, tomato, green pepper and the bay leaves from the marinade.

Grill over a charcoal fire for about 5 minutes on either side, brushing frequently with the marinade.

Serve hot, garnished with sprigs of rocket and accompanied with the dressing.

Uskumru Dolması

Mackerel stuffed with nuts and spices

One of the most inspired dishes to be found in Istanbul, this recipe epitomises the Turkish love of eating anything stuffed. It may take a little practice to perfect the art of removing the flesh from the fish but once mastered the final result is destined to provide a definite 'wow' factor at any dinner table. The mackerel are gutted through the gills and neck without slitting them open or removing the head. The flesh is then eased out of the skin and combined with nuts and spices before being stuffed back into the fish.

Serves 6
Preparation time - 40 minutes
Cooking time - 15 minutes

6 whole large mackerel, scales removed
4 eggs, beaten
plain flour
breadcrumbs or semolina
olive oil
lemon wedges to serve
parsley for garnish

For the stuffing -
3 onions, finely chopped
4 tablespoons pine nut kernels
4 tablespoons currants
4 tablespoons roughly ground walnuts
1/2 teaspoon ground cinnamon
1/2 teaspoon ground allspice
salt and pepper to taste
1/4 cup chopped dill
1/4 cup chopped parsley

To prepare the fish, remove the gills and through this opening remove the guts. Rinse well and roll each one backward and forward on a board to loosen the inner flesh. Without breaking the skin, snap the backbone just short of the tail and then again at the head. Through the opening of the gills take hold of the backbone and ease it up and down gently before drawing it out. Work the fish between thumb and forefinger to loosen the inner flesh, remove, check carefully for bones, chop and put to one side. Rinse the mackerel well, dry and put aside.

For the stuffing, heat some olive oil in a pan and soften the onions. Add the nuts, currants and spices and then the mackerel flesh. Season with salt and pepper and cook gently for about 3 minutes. Allow to cool slightly and add the chopped dill and parsley.

Gently stuff the empty fish with the stuffing. Dip in flour, beaten egg and finally breadcrumbs. Fry in olive oil until brown on both sides. Allow to cool, serve sliced diagonally to reveal the stuffing, garnish with parsley and serve with lemon wedges to squeeze over.

Asma Yaprağında Sardalya

Grilled sardines wrapped in vine leaves

When the grapevine leaves are plentiful and sardines in season, this dish constitutes a harmonious marriage of resources from land and sea. If using fresh vine leaves, blanch first in boiling water and then plunge into cold to preserve the taste and colour. If they are difficult to find, use the preserved variety but be sure to soak them before use in hot water to remove the brine.

Serves 4 - 6
Preparation time - 25 minutes
Cooking time - 10 minutes

12 whole sardines
(cleaned and gills removed)
12 grapevine leaves
grapevine leaves for the grill

For the marinade -
juice of 1 lemon
1/2 cup olive oil
salt to taste

For the dressing -
juice of 1 lemon
olive oil
salt to taste
chopped parsley

Without removing the heads and tails or breaking the skin, snap the backbone just short of the tail, then again at the head and carefully remove it through the opening of the gills. Rinse well and dry.

Combine the ingredients of the marinade, add the fish and set aside for 15-30 minutes. Mix together the ingredients for the dressing.

Wrap each sardine in a grapevine leaf. Brush the extra leaves with the marinade, place on the grill and when hot and smouldering add the wrapped fish with the openings of the leaves face down.

Cook for about 5 minutes on both sides. Serve hot from the grill with the dressing and freshly toasted bread.

Sardalya Tuzlama

Sardines pickled in lemon and salt

In many Turkish fish restaurants you are likely to come across delicious fish dishes served in small portions as appetizers or meze. With this particular dish, marinating the fish with salt and lemon means there is no need to cook it, therefore harnessing all the full flavour and goodness. Any fish in season can be prepared in this way.

Serves 4
Preparation time - 15 minutes

500g/1.1 lb fresh sardine fillets
juice of 2 lemons
salt
olive oil
sprigs of rocket
lemon wedges to serve

Arrange the fish in layers in a dish, sprinkling some salt and lemon juice between each layer.

Cover with cling film and refrigerate for 2-3 days.

Serve drizzled with olive oil, accompanied with sprigs of rocket or dill and lemon wedges to squeeze over.

Balık Köftesi

Fish croquettes

Fish *köfte* are a great favourite in the country's largest seaside cities Istanbul and Izmir. Typically bonito is used, but grey mullet and sea bass work equally well. This is the most perfect way to use up left over fish and any combination of herbs and spices can be used.

Serves 4
Preparation time - 30 minutes
Cooking time - 15 minutes

2 whole bonitos (450g/1lb)
bay leaves, black peppercorns, lemon juice
1/2 cup parsley, chopped (stalks reserved)
1 onion, cut in half
2 slices stale bread
4 eggs, beaten
1/2 teaspoon cumin or allspice

1 tablespoon pine nut kernels
1 tablespoon currants
salt and pepper to taste
plain white flour
dried breadcrumbs
sunflower oil for frying
lemon wedges to serve

Poach the fish whole in a little water with half the onion, a few bay leaves, peppercorns, the stalks of the parsley and a squeeze of lemon. Remove the fish, allow to cool, flake away the cooked flesh and put to one side.

Remove the crusts of the bread, soak in water, squeeze dry and crumble into a bowl. Add 2 of the beaten eggs, chopped parsley, pine nuts, currants, the remaining half onion grated, allspice or cumin, the flaked fish and season with salt and pepper.

Thoroughly knead all the ingredients together. Taking a spoonful at a time, working with wet hands, form into balls and then roll into finger shapes. Dip these in flour, then the remaining beaten egg and finally dried breadcrumbs.

Fry in hot oil until brown and crispy. Serve hot with lemon wedges to squeeze over.

Karides Güveç

Tomato, pepper and prawn casserole

Portions are individually cooked in little earthenware or terracotta pots. Add as much garlic and any combination of fresh chopped herbs as you wish and be sure to have plenty of fresh crusty bread to mop up the delicious juice. This dish can be served either as a starter or as a main course.

Serves 6
Preparation time - 30 minutes
Cooking time - 15 minutes

1kg/2lbs fresh prawns or shrimps
3 tomatoes, skinned, seeds removed and chopped
3 small green bell peppers, seeds removed and chopped
1/2 cup fresh dill and parsley, chopped
1 onion, chopped
4 garlic cloves, sliced
olive oil
salt and freshly ground black pepper
125g/5oz hard yellow cheese, grated

Peel and clean the prawns, removing the digestive tract if necessary. Dry well on absorbent kitchen paper, put in a bowl and sprinkle a little salt over.

Heat a little olive oil and sauté the onion and garlic until soft. Add this to the prawns, stir in half the fresh herbs, the chopped tomatoes and green peppers and season with freshly ground black pepper.

Divide the mixture between ovenproof bowls and top with the grated cheese. Bake in a hot oven for 15-20 minutes. Serve immediately, sprinkled with the remaining fresh herbs.

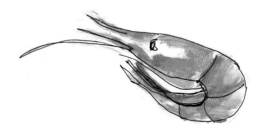

Midye Pilaki

Mussels stewed with vegetables and garlic

Mussels are plentiful in Turkish waters, especially the Bosphorus. This dish is traditionally enjoyed cold as an appetiser or as part of a big fish feast.

Serves 4 - 6
Preparation time - 20 minutes
Cooking time - 35 minutes

40 mussels, shells and beards removed
1/2 cup olive oil
1 onion, chopped
1 carrot, diced
1 potato, diced
1 small celeriac, diced, leaves chopped

4 garlic cloves, sliced
1 teaspoon salt
1 teaspoon sugar
2 tomatoes, chopped
1/2 cup parsley, chopped
lemon wedges to squeeze over

Bring 3 cups of water to the boil. Add the mussels and blanch for about 3 minutes. Drain the mussels, reserving the cooking liquid, and set aside.

Heat the olive oil, add the onions and cook until soft. Add the carrots and when they begin to soften, add the potatoes, celeriac, the leaves and garlic. Continue cooking until all the vegetables are translucent. Add the salt, sugar, tomatoes and 2 cups of the reserved cooking liquid. Continue cooking until the vegetables are tender and the cooking liquid is almost absorbed. Add more of the liquid if required.

Add the mussels and half the chopped parsley, bring to simmering point and then allow to cool.

Serve garnished with the remaining chopped parsley and lemon wedges to squeeze over.

Hamsi Buğulama

Poached Black Sea anchovies with fresh herbs

One of the many favourite *hamsi* dishes, this method of poaching fish can also be used for red mullet, horse mackerel and sardines.

Serves 4 - 6
Preparation time - 10 minutes
Cooking time - 10 minutes

1kg/2lbs small fish fillets
1/4 cup olive oil
2 tomatoes, chopped
4 spring onions, finely chopped
1/2 cup chopped parsley
1/2 cup chopped dill
salt and freshly ground black pepper
1 lemon, thinly sliced

Dry the fish on absorbent kitchen paper. Mix together the olive oil, tomatoes, spring onions and herbs. Season with salt and freshly ground black pepper and lay half the mixture in a shallow pan. Lay the fish on top and cover with the remaining mixture. Cover with slices of lemon and add enough hot water to just cover the fish. Cover and cook on a moderate heat for 7-10 minutes depending on the size of the fish. Alternatively bake in a moderate oven.

Serve with freshly baked bread as part of a meze spread.

Kağıtta Levrek

Sea bass baked in paper parcels

Levrek is now farmed intensively in Turkey, but the wild version is distinctly tastier. This method can be used with any firm-fleshed fish and with any combination of vegetables and herbs. The individual portions of fish steam perfectly in their own parcels, which are then served at the table. Fish steaks also work just as well, but may need a little longer to cook than fillets. Any fish can be cooked in this way.

Serves 6
Preparation time - 20 minutes
Cooking time - 30 minutes

6 sea bass fillets
1 onion, finely sliced
6 large mushrooms, thinly sliced
2 green bell peppers, seeds removed and thinly sliced
4 tomatoes, chopped

2 bay leaves
juice of 1 lemon
salt and freshly ground black pepper
melted butter
2 tablespoons chopped dill

Sauté the onion, mushrooms and green pepper in a little butter. Add the tomatoes, bay leaves and lemon juice, season with salt and pepper and cook gently for about 10 minutes.

Cut 6 pieces of greaseproof paper approximately 20cmx40cm/8inx16in. Brush one side with melted butter and fold over in half lengthways. Fold over the edges on each side twice, creating a bag and leaving an opening.

Place in each bag a fish fillet. Spoon in the vegetables, sprinkle in the chopped dill and fold over the open ends to seal. Brush the bags with a little water and bake in a moderate oven for 15-20 minutes.

Serve immediately in the bags, slashed open to reveal the fish within.

Barbunya Tava

Pan-fried red mullet

What must be the most delicately sweet fish, there is little more you should do with red mullet than this.
Fresh into the pan and eaten immediately with a simple salad and a glass of crisp
white wine…holiday heaven!

Serves 4
Preparation time - 5 minutes
Cooking time - 5 minutes

1kg/2.2lbs red mullet, cleaned and gutted
2 eggs, beaten
plain white flour
salt and freshly ground black pepper
sunflower oil for frying
parsley or rocket leaves for garnish
lemon wedges to squeeze over

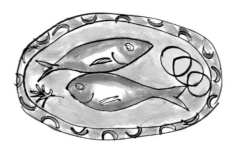

Dry the fish well on absorbent kitchen paper. Dip in beaten egg and then in flour seasoned with a little salt and black pepper.
Heat the oil and fry on either side until golden brown.

Drain on absorbent kitchen paper and serve hot, garnished with parsley or rocket and lemon wedges to squeeze over.

Taratorlu Midye Tava

Deep-fried mussels in beer batter with garlic and walnut sauce

In Istanbul, one experience not to be missed is picking up midye tava from one of the many vendors serving them hot from the pan. Traditionally they are served with *tarator* – a sauce made from garlic and crushed walnuts.

Serves 8
Preparation time - 20 minutes
Cooking time - 10 minutes

40 mussels, shells and beards removed
2 cups plain white flour
11/2 cups of lager or beer
salt
sunflower oil to fry

For the tarator sauce -
3 slices of stale bread
5 cloves garlic
2 tablespoons vinegar
1/2 cup ground walnuts
1 tablespoon olive oil

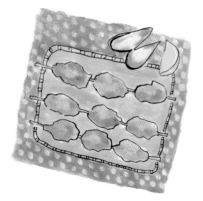

To make the tarator sauce, remove the crusts of the bread and soak in water. Squeeze the bread dry and crumble into a bowl with the other ingredients for the sauce. Using a food processor, blitz until smooth and set aside.

Dry the mussels thoroughly and dredge in half the flour. Mix the remaining flour with the beer and a little salt until you have a smooth batter.

In a deep-sided pan heat the oil. Dip the mussels in the batter and fry until golden brown, taking care not to overload the pan.

Drain on absorbent kitchen paper and serve immediately, pierced on wooden cocktail sticks with the accompanying tarator sauce.

Note – There are variations of tarator depending on region. In the Aegean, almonds are more plentiful, in the Black Sea region hazelnuts and in Central Anatolia walnuts.

Tuzda Balık

Fish baked in a salt crust

This dish never ceases to impress. The fish is cooked in the oven encased in a salt crust, which enables the fish to stay moist and succulent. The hardened salt is then cracked open and the top layer removed to reveal the fish within. Any thick-skinned fish, such as sea bass can be used, though it should always be fresh and of a reasonable size. Serve as a main course with an accompanying green salad.

Serves 4
Preparation time - 10 minutes
Cooking time - 60 minutes

1 large sea bass
sea salt
parsley for garnish
lemon wedges to squeeze over

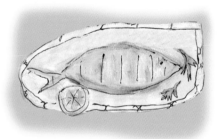

Preheat oven to 190c/370f/gas mark 5.

Leaving the fish whole, remove the scales and guts. Wash thoroughly and dry with absorbent kitchen paper.

Cover the bottom of a baking tray with a thick layer of salt. Compress this with the heel of your hand. Lay the fish on top and cover with another thick layer of salt, pressing it hard to completely encase the fish.

Place in the oven for between 45-60 minutes, depending on the size of the fish.

To serve, crack the salt crust open with a hard object, removing the top layer of salt and the skin of the fish with it. Garnish with parsley and lemon wedges to squeeze over.

Fırında Palamut Pilaki

Oven baked bonito with vegetables and garlic

Absolutely any fish can be cooked in this way... turbot, sea bass, grey mullet. If you wish, replace some of the fluid with white wine and use as much garlic as you like.

Serves 4
Preparation time - 20 minutes
Cooking time - 40 minutes

1 whole bonito, cleaned and gutted
1/4 cup olive oil
1 onion, thinly sliced
1 carrot, thinly sliced
1 small potato, diced
1 small celeriac, diced, leaves chopped
4 garlic cloves, sliced
1 teaspoon sugar

1 teaspoon salt
freshly ground black pepper
2 tomatoes, chopped
1/2 teaspoon paprika (optional)
1/2 cup chopped parsley
1 lemon, sliced thinly
juice of 1/2 lemon

Preheat oven to 180c/350f/gas mark 4.

For this dish, the fish can be filleted or sliced into steaks without cutting through the backbone, and leaving the head and tail intact. It can then be arranged as a whole fish in the oven dish. Dry well and sprinkle with a little salt.

Heat the olive oil. Add the onions and cook until soft. Add the carrots and cook until they start to soften. Add the potatoes, celeriac, the leaves and garlic. When the vegetables are all translucent add the salt, sugar, tomatoes and 2 cups of water. Continue cooking until the vegetables are nearly tender and the cooking liquid is almost absorbed.

Spread half the vegetables in an oven proof dish. Place the fish on top and then cover with the remaining vegetables, half the chopped parsley, the optional paprika and season with freshly ground black pepper. Place the lemon slices on top and pour the lemon juice over.

Cover and bake in a moderate oven for about 20 minutes or until the fish is tender.

Sprinkle over the remaining chopped parsley and serve immediately.

Hamsi Tava

Deep fried crispy Black Sea anchovies

Another of the many *hamsi* dishes, some Black Sea establishments specialise in these delicious little fish cooked this way and accompanied, of course, with *rakı* - a perfect combination!

Serves 4 - 6
Preparation time - 10 minutes
Cooking time - 20

1kg/2.2lbs fresh anchovies, cleaned
2 eggs, beaten
plain white flour/cornmeal
salt and black pepper
sunflower oil for frying
lemon wedges to squeeze over

Dip the fish in the beaten egg and then dredge in seasoned flour or corn meal. Fry until crispy, taking care not to overload the pan.

Drain on absorbent kitchen paper.

Serve hot as an appetizer with a squeeze of lemon.

Fırında Lüfer Buğulama

Oven poached blue fish in a garlic and tomato sauce

Any fish can be poached in this way and it can be cooked on the stovetop if you prefer. White wine or fish stock can be used to create a richer sauce, and be as generous with the garlic as you wish. Use fish fillets or steaks, or for a more traditional effect leave the fish whole.

Serves 4
Preparation time - 20 minutes
Cooking time - 40 minutes

4 whole bluefish, cleaned and gutted
6 tablespoons butter
2 onions, sliced into half moons
2 green bell peppers, sliced
6 large mushrooms, sliced
4 garlic cloves, sliced
6 large ripe tomatoes, chopped

1/4 teaspoon sugar
4 bay leaves
2 cups water/fish stock/white wine
salt and freshly ground black pepper
1 lemon, thinly sliced
chopped parsley for garnish

Preheat oven to 180c/350f/gas mark 4.

Dry the fish well and sprinkle with a little salt. Heat the butter and soften the onions. Add the peppers, mushrooms, garlic and cook for 2 minutes. Then add the tomatoes, sugar, bay leaves, water, stock or wine and season with salt and freshly ground black pepper. Cook until slightly reduced.

Place the fish in a well-buttered oven-proof dish, cover with the tomato mixture and top with the slices of lemon. Bake in a moderate oven for 15-20 minutes or until the fish is tender.

Sprinkle with chopped parsley and serve immediately.

Ahtapot Salatası

Octopus salad

Octopus makes a mouthwatering salad. In Turkey it is very popular in seaside tavernas served as a meze. Octopus spend the winter in deep waters and in spring move to shallow coastal areas.

Serves 4 - 6
Preparation time - 10 minutes
Cook time - 2 hours

1 octopus (1kg/2.2lbs)
1/2 cup vinegar
2 teaspoons salt
1 teaspoon sugar
6 bay leaves
10 pepper corns
1 bunch of parsley
juice of 1 lemon
olive oil
lemon wedges to serve

Put the octopus in a large pan. Add the vinegar, sugar and salt, bay leaves and peppercorns. Strip the leaves from the parsley and add the stalks. Chop the leaves and put aside for garnish. Add about 3 cups of water and cook on a low heat until tender, approximately 2 hours, depending on the size.

Drain and, when cool enough to handle, rinse and cut the octopus into bite-size pieces, removing the outer gelatinous red skin if you wish.

Toss in olive oil and lemon, season with a little salt and pepper and serve cold, garnished with chopped parsley.

Note - If you are unlucky enough to buy an octopus that hasn't been tenderised… in other words beaten to a pulp on the rocks, don't despair. Deep-freeze for 2 days prior to cooking. It will come out marvellously tender.

Midye Dolması

Aromatic rice stuffed mussels

Istanbul and Izmir are famous for their stuffed mussels. Street vendors serve aromatic rice filled, mouth-watering mussels in their shells with lemon to squeeze over. This recipe stuffs approximately 20 mussels. And don't worry if there is stuffing left over, you can use it to stuff a vegetable or two! (page 41).

Serves 4 - 6
Preparation time - 30 minutes
Cook time - 25 minutes

For the stuffing -
1/2 cup rice
1 tablespoon currants
4 tablespoons olive oil
1 tablespoon pine nut kernels
2 onions, finely chopped
1/2 teaspoon ground cinnamon
1/2 teaspoon allspice
1/2 teaspoon black pepper
1/2 teaspoon salt
1/2 teaspoon sugar
chopped fresh mint, parsley and dill

For the mussels -
20-25 fresh large mussels, cleaned
1 onion, sliced
1/4 teaspoon sugar
1/4 teaspoon salt
1 cup hot water
1/4 cup olive oil
1 lemon, cut in slices
chopped parsley for garnish
lemon wedges to squeeze over

Opening each mussel shell carefully with a sharp knife and taking care not to pull each section of the shell apart, cut away the hairy beard, wash well and drain.

Soak the rice and currants in hot, salted water for 30 minutes, rinse thoroughly until the water runs clear and drain. Meanwhile, heat the oil and lightly brown the pine nuts. Add the onion and cook until soft. Add the drained rice and currants and stir to ensure the grains are well coated. Add the remaining ingredients for the stuffing, except the herbs. Add enough hot water just to cover the rice, cover and cook until the moisture has been absorbed. Pour the rice into a large bowl to cool and incorporate the chopped herbs.

Spoon into each mussel some of the rice stuffing. Don't overstuff, as the rice will expand slightly during the cooking time. Close the shells tightly.

Put the sliced onions in a pan and place the mussels carefully on top in layers. Whisk together the water, salt, sugar and olive oil and pour over the mussels. Arrange the lemon slices on top and cover with a wet piece of greaseproof paper. On top put a plate, which will act as a weight. Cover and cook over a medium heat for approximately 30 minutes or until the shells are opening as the rice expands. Leave covered and put aside to cool. To serve, brush the shells with oil, sprinkle with chopped parsley and decorate with lemon wedges to squeeze over.

Pilavlar ve Hamur İşleri
Pilafs and Savoury Pastries

Pilafs and savoury pastries are an intrinsic part of Turkish cuisine. A successful pilaf is the sign of a great cook; huge round trays specially designed for baking pies (*börek*), concealing mouth-watering fillings is a standard feature in all Turkish kitchens.

During their migration from central Asia, pastoral nomads used unleavened dough to make flat breads cooked on metal griddles over evening campfires. Over the centuries this dough has evolved into what we know today as *yufka,* dough rolled out with a long thin rolling pin to make round paper-thin sheets of pastry used to make many forms of *börek*.

In the 10th century, Selçuk Turks, descendants of the earlier Turkic nomads, began to settle in the fertile areas of Anatolia and sow crops of grain. The Persians introduced them to pilafs and various new fruits and nuts. Rice dishes gained popularity and the Ottomans continued to develop them in the palace kitchens, favouring long grain rice for pilafs, and shorter grains for stuffing *dolma* and making milk puddings.

Rice is one of the few ingredients used in the Turkish kitchen that doesn't grow abundantly in Turkey and therefore most rural families in wheat growing regions tend to eat more *bulgur* pilafs, reserving rice pilafs for special celebrations.

Beyaz Pilav

White rice pilaf with currants and pine nuts

Rice originally came from China and greatly influenced Indian and later Persian cuisine during the time that the great silk trading routes opened throughout Asia. Although it has become very much a part of everyday Turkish cuisine, it was originally only enjoyed by the wealthy. Pine nuts and currants are used in this recipe, though quite commonly you will find plain white pilafs combined with şehriye (vermicelli).

Serves 6
Preparation time - 10 minutes
Cooking time - 20 minutes

2 cups long grain rice   **4 cups of chicken stock**
2 tablespoons currants   **(stock cubes can be used)**
2 tablespoons pine nuts   **1 teaspoon salt**
4 tablespoons butter   **1/2 teaspoon sugar**
    finely chopped parsley for garnish

Soak the rice and currants in hot salted water for 30 minutes. Rinse under cold running water, drain and set aside.

In a large pan gently sauté the pine nuts in the butter until golden. Add the chicken stock, salt and sugar and when it starts to simmer add the rice and currants. Stir once and cover. Cook over a medium heat for about 10 minutes or until all the stock has been absorbed and steam holes appear in the surface of the rice. It is important not to stir the rice during this time. Turn down the heat as low as possible and continue cooking for a further 3-5 minutes.

Remove from the heat, cover the top of the pan with a cloth or absorbant kitchen paper and replace the lid. The rice will continue cooking in the steam and the cloth will absorb any excess moisture. Leave to stand, covered, for at least 20 minutes before serving.

Fluff up the rice with a fork and serve hot, garnished with chopped parsley.

Note - To make a rice pilaf with vermicelli, use 2 tablespoons of vermicelli instead of the pine nuts and leave out the currants.

Domatesli Pilav

Tomato rice pilaf

This tangy flavoured rice is dependent on tasty, sun-kissed Mediterranean tomatoes. However, you can substitute canned chopped tomatoes and still get a good result.

Serves 6
Preparation time - 15 minutes
Cooking time - 30 minutes

2 cups long grain rice	**1 teaspoon salt**
1 small onion, finely chopped	**1/2 teaspoon sugar**
4 tablespoons butter	**4 cups meat stock (stock cubes can be used)**
4 tomatoes, skinned, and finely chopped	**finely chopped parsley for garnish**

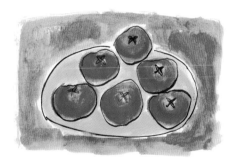

Soak the rice in hot salted water for 30 minutes. Rinse under cold running water, drain and set aside.

In a large pan sauté the onion in the butter until soft. Add the tomatoes and cook for a further 5 minutes. Add the salt, sugar and stock and when it starts to simmer add the rice, stir once and cover. Cook gently for about 10 minutes or until the stock is absorbed and steam holes appear in the surface of the rice. It is important not to stir the rice during this time. Turn down the heat as low as possible and continue cooking for a further 3-5 minutes.

Remove from the heat, cover the top of the pan with a cloth or absorbant kitchen paper and replace the lid. The rice will continue cooking in the steam and the cloth will absorb any excess moisture. Leave to stand covered for at least 20 minutes before serving.

Fluff up the rice with a fork and serve hot, garnished with chopped parsley.

İzmir Pilavı

Aromatic pilaf with fruit and nuts

This is a pilaf inspired by the inhabitants of ancient Smyrna, present day Izmir. Enriched with fruit and nuts and cooked with olive oil, it makes a great option served cold as a delicious rice salad.

Serves 4
Preparation time - 10 minutes
Cooking time - 30 minutes

1 cup long grain rice	2 tablespoons walnuts or
2 tablespoons currants	blanched almonds, coarsely chopped
2 tablespoons olive oil	1/2 teaspoon ground cinnamon
1 onion, finely chopped	1 teaspoon salt
2 tablespoons pine nuts	1/2 teaspoon sugar
2 cups hot chicken stock	freshly ground black pepper to taste
(stock cubes can be used)	finely chopped parsley for garnish
2 Turkish dried apricots, thinly sliced	

Soak the rice and currants in hot salted water for 30 minutes. Rinse under cold running water, drain and set aside.

In a large pan, heat the oil over a gentle heat and sauté the onion together with the pine nuts until the onion is soft and the pine nuts lightly brown. Add the stock and apricot slices and bring to the boil. Add the walnuts or blanched almonds, cinnamon, rice, currants, salt, sugar and black pepper. Stir once and cover. Cook over a medium heat for about 10 minutes or until the stock is absorbed and steam holes appear in the surface of the rice. It is important not to stir the rice during this time. Turn down the heat as low as possible and continue cooking for a further 3-5 minutes.

Remove from the heat, cover the top of the pan with a cloth or absorbant kitchen paper and replace the lid. The rice will continue cooking in the steam and the cloth will absorb any excess moisture. Leave to stand covered for at least 20 minutes before serving.

Fluff up the pilaf with a fork and serve hot, garnished with parsley.

İç Pilav

Oriental aromatic rice pilaf

The Ottoman court provided lots of opportunity for creativity in the kitchen and many chefs were eager to please the sultan and gain promotion. This rich pilaf, literally 'interior pilaf', was highly successful and became popular used as stuffing for vegetables and poultry. Use it to stuff traditional roast turkey or chicken or just as it is, as an accompaniment to grilled meats.

Serves 6
Preparation time - 15 minutes
Cooking time - 35 minutes

2 cups long grain rice
3 tablespoons currants
4 level tablespoons butter
3 tablespoons pine nuts
1 onion, finely chopped
225g/8oz chicken livers, diced
1/2 teaspoon ground allspice

1/2 teaspoon ground cinnamon
1 teaspoon salt
1/2 teaspoon sugar
4 cups hot chicken stock (stock cubes can be used)
freshly ground black pepper
1/2 cup of chopped dill, mint and parsley

Soak the rice and currants in hot salted water for 30 minutes. Rinse under cold running water, drain and set aside.

In a large pan, gently sauté the pine nuts in the butter until golden. Add the onion and cook until soft. Stir in the livers and when lightly browned, add the rice and currants. Continue cooking and stir well to ensure the rice grains are evenly coated. Add the spices, sugar, salt and the hot chicken stock, bring to the boil, stir once and cover. Continue to cook over a medium heat for about 10 minutes or until the stock is absorbed and steam holes appear in the surface of the rice. It is important not to stir the rice during this time. Turn down the heat as low as possible and continue cooking for a further 3-5 minutes.

Remove from the heat, cover the top of the pan with a cloth or absorbant kitchen paper and replace the lid. The rice will continue cooking in the steam and the cloth will absorb any excess moisture. Leave to stand covered for at least 20 minutes before serving.

Season with freshly ground black pepper. Add the herbs and combine into the pilaf. Serve hot with roast lamb, chicken or turkey.

Hamsili Pilav

Baked hamsi pilaf

Hamsi are a type of anchovy found in abundance along Turkey's Black Sea coast. For many families of this region they are of great dietary importance. They are often simply dipped in flour, fried and eaten whole. They can be found in *köfte*, *börek*, *dolma*, and even work their way into desserts. This dramatic pilaf, encased with fish, is a great favourite throughout Turkey. Sprats or small sardines can be substituted for the *hamsi* and ground sumac makes an interesting garnish.

Serves 6
Preparation time - 25 minutes
Cooking time - 40 minutes

**1kg/2.2lbs hamsi
(heads removed and filleted)
2 cups long grain rice
3 tablespoons currants
4 tablespoons butter
1 medium onion, finely chopped
3 tablespoons pine nuts**

**1 teaspoon dried mint
1/2 teaspoon ground allspice
1/2 teaspoon ground cinnamon
1 teaspoon salt
1/2 teaspoon sugar
4 cups hot water
1/4 cup finely chopped parsley**

**1/4 cup finely chopped dill
freshly ground black pepper
extra butter for greasing and drizzling
ground sumac for garnish
lemon wedges to serve**

Preheat oven to 200c/400f/gas mark 6.

Soak the rice and currants in hot salted water for 30 minutes. Rinse thoroughly in cold running water, drain and set aside. Lay out the prepared hamsi, skin side down, on absorbent kitchen paper and sprinkle with a little salt and set aside.

In a large pan, sauté the onion and pine nuts in the butter. When the onions are soft and the pine nuts golden, add the rice and stir to ensure the rice grains are evenly coated. Add the mint, allspice, cinnamon, salt and sugar and stir well. Add the hot water and bring to the boil, stir once and cover. Cook on a medium heat for about 10 minutes or until the water is absorbed and steam holes appear in the surface of the rice. It is important not to stir the rice during this time. Turn down the heat as low as possible and continue cooking for a further 3-5 minutes. Remove from the heat, cover the top of the pan with a cloth or absorbant kitchen paper and replace the lid. The rice will continue cooking in the steam and the cloth will absorb any excess moisture. Set aside to cool.

Meanwhile, generously grease with butter, a glass circular ovenproof dish (large enough to accommodate the rice). Starting at the top, allowing the first row to hang over the edge, line the dish with the hamsi in a single layer, placing the skin sides against the outer edge of the dish. Carefully place them lengthways, side by side, to create a radial pattern working towards the base of the dish. The final result is to have the pilaf completely encased with fish. Set aside some of the fish to place on top.

Add the chopped parsley and dill to the rice, season with freshly ground black pepper and combine well. Pour the rice into the fish lined dish, level it out and fold over the fish hanging over the edges. Use the remaining fish, placing them skin side up to cover the surface of the rice. Drizzle over a little more melted butter. Place the dish upright in the preheated oven and bake for 20-25 minutes.

Remove from the oven and turn upside down on a serving plate. Leave to stand for a few minutes and then ease the pilaf out gently. Garnish with a sprinkling of sumac and serve hot with lemon wedges to squeeze over.

Bulgur Pilavı

Bulgur wheat pilaf

Often confused with cracked wheat, *bulgur* wheat is a grain made from cooked whole wheat berries, which have had the bran removed, and are then dried in the sun and crushed. As it has already been cooked, it requires little or no cooking. It is available coarsely and finely ground. For pilaf, the coarser type is used to create a nutty and delicious dish, which is a meal in itself when served with yogurt. *Bulgur* is a major staple in many rural areas of Turkey.

Serves 6
Preparation time - 10 minutes
Cooking time - 20 minutes

2 cups of coarse bulgur wheat
1 onion, finely chopped
4 tablespoons butter
1 green bell pepper, diced
4 tomatoes, chopped
1 tablespoon tomato paste

2 cups hot meat or chicken stock
(stock cubes can be used)
1 teaspoon salt
1/2 teaspoon sugar
freshly ground black pepper
chopped parsley for garnish

Rinse the bulgur under cold running water, drain and set aside.

Sauté the chopped onions in butter until soft. Add the chopped green pepper and tomatoes and cook for a further 5 minutes. Add the tomato paste and meat stock, and bring to the boil.

Add the bulgur, salt, sugar, ground black pepper and stir once. Cover and cook over a low heat until the bulgur has absorbed all the stock and steam holes are visable on the surface. It is important not to stir the pilaf during this time. Remove from the heat, cover the pan with a cloth or absorbant kitchen paper and replace the lid. The bulgur will continue cooking in the steam and the cloth will absorb any excess moisture. Leave to stand, covered, for at least 20 minutes before serving.

Fluff up the pilaf with a fork and serve hot, garnished with a sprinkling of chopped parsley.

Patlıcanlı İç Pilav

Aromatic aubergine pilaf

This is one of the many dishes to come from the Ottoman palace kitchens to satisfy the sultans' cravings for more aubergines. Forty different dishes were concocted to satisfy their demands. This pilaf, accompanied with creamy yogurt infused with garlic, is a meal in itself. Cooked using olive oil, it also makes a great cold rice salad.

Serves 4 - 6
Preparation time - 20 minutes
Cook time - 25 minutes

1 cup long grain rice	**1/2 teaspoon sugar**
1 tablespoon currants	**1/2 teaspoon ground cinnamon**
2 aubergines	**1/2 teaspoon ground allspice**
4 tablespoons olive oil	**1 tomato, skinned, seeds removed and chopped**
1 tablespoon pine nuts	**2 cups hot water**
1 onion, finely chopped	**1/2 cup of freshly chopped mint, parsley and dill**
1 teaspoon salt	**freshly ground black pepper**

Soak the rice and currants in hot salted water for 30 minutes, rinse under cold running water, drain and set aside. Meanwhile with a sharp peeler, partially peel the aubergines in alternate vertical stripes from stem to base and cut away the stalk. Soak in salted water for 30 minutes, drain and squeeze dry. Cut into small cubes.

Heat 2 tablespoons of olive oil and sauté the aubergines with a little salt and sugar until soft. Remove with a straining spoon and set aside to drain on absorbent kitchen paper.

In a large pan, sauté the pine nuts and chopped onions in the rest of the olive oil, until the pine nuts are golden and the onions soft. Add the drained rice and currants, and stir to ensure the grains are evenly coated. Add the salt, sugar, spices, chopped tomato and 2 cups of hot water. Bring to the boil, stir once and cover. Cook on a medium heat, for about 10 minutes or until the water is absorbed and steam holes appear in the surface of the rice. It is important not to stir the rice during this time. Turn down the heat as low as possible and continue cooking for a further 3-5 minutes.

Remove from the heat, add the aubergine and cover the top of the pan with a cloth or absorbant kitchen paper and replace the lid. The rice will continue cooking in the steam and the cloth will absorb any excess moisture. Leave to stand, covered for at least 20 minutes before serving. Season with freshly ground black pepper, add the herbs and incorporate them and the aubergines evenly through the pilaf with a fork.

Serve immediately whilst still hot, or cold as a salad.

Mantı

Meat stuffed dumplings with garlicky yogurt and paprika butter

Mantı is a dish believed to have been inspired by the Chinese. Served with yogurt, it is now very much a Turkish hallmark. The dough is made and rolled out extremely thinly with an *oklava* – a long thin rolling pin. If you don't have one, a good substitute is a long thin wooden curtain pole.

Serves 6
Preparation time - 60 minutes
Cooking time – 15-45 minutes

For the dough -
2 1/2 cups plain white flour
1 teaspoon salt
1 egg
4 tablespoons cold water
3 tablespoons sunflower oil

For the filling -
225g/8oz minced beef or lamb
1 onion, grated
2 tablespoons finely chopped parsley
salt and freshly ground black pepper
(to taste)

To cook -
6 cups/1.5 litres meat stock
(stock cubes can be used)

The accompanying sauce -
4 cups/1kg natural creamy yogurt
4 garlic cloves, crushed in salt
4 tablespoons melted butter
2 teaspoons paprika
dried mint (optional)

Sift the flour into a bowl and add the salt. Make a well in the middle and add the egg, water and oil. Draw in the flour and work everything together to make a dough. Place on a floured surface and work until the dough is smooth and elastic. Oil the bowl, return the dough and cover with a damp cloth. Leave to rest for 1 hour at room temperature.

Meanwhile, mix together the ingredients for the filling and season with salt and black pepper.

For the accompanying sauce, combine the yogurt and garlic and whisk until smooth. Melt the butter, add the paprika and remove from the heat when it starts to sizzle.

On a well-floured surface knead the dough for 5 minutes. Divide it into two pieces; cover one with the damp cloth and on a well-floured surface, roll out the other half with a long thin rolling pin. Roll out the dough as thinly as possible. Cut in strips 5cm/2in wide and again in the opposite direction at the same width to create squares. These squares can be made smaller if you wish, but this size is manageable. Wet the edges of the pastry squares and spoon a teaspoon of filling onto the centre of each one. Pick up each square by the 4 corners, pinch together firmly and seal closed. Place on a well-floured surface and then continue using the second half of dough in the same way.

Boiling method – In a pan, heat the meat stock and when boiling add the mantı carefully and cook for about 15 minutes or until they rise to the surface.
Baking method – Place the prepared mantı in a well-oiled baking pan. Bake in a moderate oven for about 20 minutes or until the edges are lightly browned. Add 4 cups of stock to the baking pan, cover, return to the oven and continue cooking until the stock is absorbed and the mantı soft.

To serve, remove the mantı with a straining spoon and transfer to heated plates. Spoon over garlicky yogurt sauce and drizzle with paprika butter. Sprinkle with optional dried mint.

Note - Another way to serve mantı is with a rich tomato sauce with a hint of mint and paprika.

Ispanaklı Peynirli Börek

Spinach and cheese pastry roll

If you have *yufka* available, this has to be the most deliciously pleasing and easy to knock-up *börek* around. Filo pastry works just as well. You don't have to stick to the suggested filling – use anything you have handy, left over mashed potato, grated cheese, herbs and paprika make good alternatives.

Serves 6
Preparation time - 15 minutes
Cooking time - 45 minutes

500g/1lb spinach leaves
200g/7oz Turkish white cheese/feta
3 eggs, beaten
2 sheets yufka/6 sheets filo pastry
olive oil/melted butter
toasted sesame seeds/nigella seeds
freshly ground black pepper

Preheat oven to 180c/350f/gas mark 4.

Remove the stalks of the spinach, wash and chop finely. Mix together in a bowl with the cheese and 2 of the beaten eggs.

Spread out 1 sheet of the pastry on a flat surface and brush with olive oil or melted butter. Fold in half and brush again. (If using filo, layer 3 sheets of pastry twice). Repeat the process with the second sheet.

Divide the filling over the two folded sheets and spread out evenly.

Roll up the pastry lengthways, incorporating the filling. Transfer carefully onto an oiled baking tray one at a time. Start with the first and coil it around itself. Continue with the second, coiling it around the first and folding the ends underneath.

Whisk together the remaining beaten egg with a little more olive oil and brush over the pastry. Sprinkle with sesame or nigella seeds.

Bake in a moderate oven for about 40 minutes or until the top is golden.

Serve hot or cold. This dish can be successfully reheated.

Note - Often inaccurately referred to in Turkey as black cumin, nigella or çörekotu is a peppery black aromatic seed, which can be used to add flavour to pastries and breads.

Lahmacun

Thin, crispy pizza with a piquant topping

The Middle Eastern countries are no strangers to versions of pizza and this is one commonly found in Turkey. The paper-thin *lahmacun* is a popular lunch time snack. Lemon is liberally squeezed over and then it is rolled up with sliced tomatoes and parsley. The perfect accompaniment is a cool glass of *ayran*, a refreshing blend of creamy yogurt, water and salt.

Serves 6
Preparation time - 45 minutes
Cook time - 25 minutes

For the dough -
1 teaspoon dried yeast
1/2 teaspoon sugar
1/2 cup lukewarm water
3 cups strong white flour
1/2 teaspoon salt
olive oil

For the topping -
1 tablespoon butter
1 onion, finely chopped
1 tomato, skinned and chopped
salt and sugar to taste
225g/8oz minced lamb
2 tablespoons tomato paste
1 teaspoon paprika flakes
squeeze of lemon juice

To serve -
slices of tomato
parsley
lemon wedges

Preheat the oven to 230c/450f/gas mark 8.

Cream together the yeast with the sugar and some of the lukewarm water. Sift the flour and the salt into a bowl, make a well in the middle and add the yeast mixture. Add a tablespoon of olive oil and a little more water and combine the flour gradually to create a firm dough, adding a little more water if required or a little more flour if it gets too sticky. Knead the dough on a floured surface for about 10 minutes or until it becomes smooth and elastic. Pour a drop of olive oil in a bowl and roll the dough in it to prevent it drying out. Cover with a damp cloth and leave for about 1 hour to prove in a warm place until it is double its size.

Meanwhile for the topping, lightly soften the onions in the butter, add the chopped tomato and cook until the liquid has been absorbed. Add salt and sugar to taste and set aside to cool. Put the meat in a bowl and add the tomato paste, paprika, lemon juice, cooked onions and tomato. Work this mixture into a paste with your hands.

Punch back the risen dough, knead for 2-3 minutes and then cut into 6 even pieces. Make each piece into a ball and then roll each ball out into very thin rounds. Place on a well oiled baking sheet. Spread a thin layer of the meat mixture over each one and leave to rest for 10 minutes.

Bake in the preheated oven for 10-15 minutes until brown and crispy.

Serve immediately, accompanied with tomatoes, parsley and lemon wedges to squeeze over, as suggested above.

Note - Divide the dough into smaller portions to make miniature lahmacun, excellent for serving as finger food at drinks parties.

Sigara Böreği

Crispy cheese and herb filled pastry rolls

It is thought that the Ottoman palace kitchens devised these tasty treats in order to tempt the precious little princes. These are cigar-shaped pastries, and more often than not are filled with the Turkish white cheese (similar to feta) mixed with herbs. They are made in large batches, stored in the fridge and then magically appear, hot and crispy, as a welcome to any visiting guests or family members. The pastry used is *yufka*, which if necessary can be substituted by filo pastry. The herbs used are parsley, mint and dill; use as you wish, individually or a mixture of what you have available. The ratio of cheese and herbs should be about equal.

Serves 6
Preparation time - 25 minutes
Cooking time - 10 minutes

2 sheets yufka/filo pastry
225g/8oz soft white Turkish cheese/feta
2 egg yolks
1 cup chopped parsley, mint and dill
salt and black pepper to taste
sunflower oil for frying

Mash together the cheese, egg yolks and herbs to form a smooth paste. Season with salt and pepper. However, if the cheese is a salty variety you may wish not to add salt.

Put one sheet of yufka on top of the other, cut equally down the centre to form four semicircles. Double up the semicircles and cut the four layers into two again. Repeat this once more ending with 16 elongated triangular pieces of pastry. (If using filo pastry, cut to form 16 elongated rectangles.) Keep the pastry covered with a damp cloth as you are working. This will help to avoid it getting too dry and less manageable.

Take one triangular piece of pastry and place a generous teaspoon of the cheese mixture at the wider end. Fold over the pastry from each side to seal in the mixture and then roll up tightly like a cigar. Wet the end with water to seal. Continue, keeping the finished ones covered with a damp cloth as you work. Refrigerate until required.

Heat the sunflower oil in a shallow pan and fry the cheese rolls over a medium heat until golden brown and crispy.

Serve hot as part of a meze spread.

Note - If preferred, the pastries can be brushed with oil and baked in a moderately hot oven for 20 minutes.

Muska Böreği

Crispy triangle packages with a piquant meat filling

Muska is the name for this triangular shaped pastry, but can also mean amulet, something to ward off evil. *Yufka* pastry is generally used, but filo pastry works just as well. The filling doesn't have to be this meaty one and the cheese filling in the previous recipe can be used if you prefer.

Serves 6
Preparation time - 25 minutes
Cooking time - 25 minutes

2 sheets yufka/filo pastry
1 tablespoon currants
225g/8oz lean minced beef
1 tablespoon butter
1 onion, grated
1 tomato, finely chopped
salt and pepper to taste
1 handful chopped parsley
sunflower oil for frying

Soak the currants in warm water until swollen and drain. In a frying pan sauté the minced beef with the butter and onion over a medium heat for about 10 minutes. Add the tomato and currants. Season with salt and pepper and continue cooking for a further 10 minutes. Add the parsley and set aside to cool.

Put one sheet of yufka on top of the other, cut equally down the centre to form four semicircles. Double up the semicircles and cut these layers into strips of 8cm/3in wide and about 24 cm/9 in. long, discarding the excess pastry. (If using filo pastry, cut the sheets into 16 elongated rectangles.) Keep the pastry covered with a damp cloth as you are working. This will help to avoid it getting too dry and less manageable.

With a strip of pastry facing lengthways away from you, spoon a tablespoon of the filling onto the nearest edge. Take the right hand corner of the strip and fold it diagonally over the filling to form a triangle. Then take the left corner and fold over diagonally again. Continue in this way to create a tightly wrapped triangle. Seal down the end with water. Continue, keeping the finished ones covered with a damp cloth as you work. Refrigerate until required.

Heat the sunflower oil in a shallow pan and fry the pastries over a medium heat until golden brown and crispy on both sides.

Serve hot as part of a meze spread.

Note - The small black currants - kuşüzümü used in the Turkish kitchen are sometimes referred to as bird grapes. They offer a little sweetness to savoury dishes.

Paçanga Böreği

Crispy triangle packages of cured beef and melted cheese

Another adaptation of the *muska böreği*, these delicious pastries use Turkish *pastırma*, dried and cured fillet of beef which is coated in a pungent mix of garlic, fenugreek, cumin and paprika. The cheese used is a *kaşar*, but if this isn't available any tasty yellow cheese that melts nicely will work. Any pastrami or spicy ham can also substitute the *pastırma*.

Serves 6
Preparation time - 20 minutes
Cooking time - 10 minutes

2 sheets yufka/filo pastry
200g/7oz pastırma
200g/7oz kaşar cheese, grated
finely chopped parsley
sunflower oil to fry

Put one sheet of yufka on top of the other, cut equally down the centre to form two semicircles. Double up the semicircles and cut these layers into strips of 8cm/3in wide. Cut these strips into equal lengths and discard the excess pastry. (If using filo pastry, cut the sheets into 16 elongated rectangles.) Keep the pastry covered with a damp cloth as you are working. This will help to avoid it getting too dry and less manageable.

With a strip of pastry facing lengthways away from you, place a piece of pastırma, a tablespoon of grated cheese and a little chopped parsley on the nearest edge. Take the right hand corner of the strip and fold it diagonally over the filling to form a triangle. Then take the left corner and fold over diagonally again. Continue in this way to create a tightly wrapped triangle. Seal down the end with water. Continue, keeping the finished ones covered with a damp cloth as you work. Refrigerate until required.

Heat the sunflower oil in a shallow pan and fry the pastries over a medium heat until golden brown and crispy on both sides.

Serve hot as part of a meze spread.

Kabaklı Tepsi Böreği

Layered savoury courgette and cheese pie baked in a tray

Use any filling of choice: meat, spinach, spicy pumpkin and potato, leeks; the list of possibilities is endless. This recipe uses courgette and cheese but you can use any combination from the other *börek* recipes featured in the book. *Yufka* is widely available and usually comes in large rounds measuring approximately 60cm/24in in diameter. Choose a baking pan half this size so the edges overhang and can be folded over the top to encase the pie. If using filo pastry you may need to double the quantity of sheets. Some Turkish experts insist yogurt should be included in the egg and milk mixture used between layers...this is up to you.

Serves 6 - 8
Preparation time - 30 minutes
Cooking time - 40 minutes

4 courgettes, grated	**salt and freshly ground black pepper to taste**
250g/9oz Turkish white cheese/feta	**5 sheets yufka/filo pastry**
3 eggs, beaten	**3 eggs**
6 spring onions, finely chopped	**1 cup melted butter/sunflower oil**
2 tablespoons chopped dill	**2 cups milk**

Preheat oven to 200c/400f/gas mark 6.

For the filling, put the grated courgettes in a colander and sprinkle with salt. Set aside for 30 minutes. Squeeze well to allow the excess water to run away. In a bowl, combine with the cheese, eggs, chopped spring onions and dill. Season with salt and freshly ground black pepper. You may wish to leave out the salt if the cheese is a salty variety.

Generously grease a baking pan. Whisk together the eggs, melted butter/oil and milk.

Lay the first sheet of yufka in the pan so that the edges are overhanging the pan equally on all sides. Brush this sheet generously with the egg mix. Tear the second sheet into strips and place these evenly in the base of the pan and brush generously with the egg mix. Lay the third sheet like the first and let the edges overhang. Spread the filling over the pastry and pour over a little egg mix. Tear sheets 4 and 5 into strips, continuing to layer as before, brushing with the egg mix. Finally, fold over the overhanging yufka to encase the pie and seal, brushing over the remaining egg mix. Leave to stand for 30 minutes to allow the yufka to absorb the moisture.

Cut into square portions and put in the preheated oven for about 40 minutes or until the top is golden brown and puffed up.

Serve directly from the pan or alternatively turn upside down onto a serving plate and serve when cold. This dish can be successfully reheated.

Note – To reduce the saltiness of Turkish white cheese, soak overnight in plenty of fresh water.

Tatlılar

Sweets and Puddings

In Turkey, the saying goes – 'eat sweet, talk sweet'. Puddings and sweets play a distinctive role in everyday life and many hold deep symbolic relevance. Special religious festivals, weddings, circumcisions, and times of family bereavement are occasions when a specific sweet or pudding is traditionally appropriate. The lists of milk-based puddings (*muhallebi*), sweet pastries (*baklava*) and various other tempting cakes and sweets are endless. They are enjoyed at any time of day or night and don't necessarily constitute the end of a meal; fresh fruit is more often preferred to cleanse the palate.

Lokum

Turkish delight

Prior to the arrival of refined sugar in the late 18th century, the Ottomans made a crude version of Turkish Delight using honey or *pekmez*, a concentrated grape syrup, and wheat flour. *Hacı Bekir*, a confectioner of the time, became famous due to his ingenious use of white sugar and corn starch and was summoned to Topkapı Palace to pioneer the development of what is today one of Turkey's hallmarks. Special recipes for variations of Turkish delight can now be found in all regions of Turkey. Dried fruits, nuts, seeds and desiccated coconut are incorporated into the luscious mouthfuls of fragrant jelly. *Sakız* (mastic gum), another ingredient revered by the sultans, can be used to create a chewier version and is a must if you are preparing rolled up versions of *lokum*. This recipe is for *sade* – plain *lokum*, delicately flavoured with fragrant rose water. However, you may wish to add shelled and chopped nuts of your choice – hazelnuts, pistachio nuts or walnuts work extremely well.

Serves 6
Preparation time - 15 minutes
Cooking time - 20 minutes

450g/1lb fine white sugar
2 cups water
1 teaspoon lemon juice
3 tablespoons rose water
6 tablespoons cornflour/cornstarch
sifted icing sugar/confectioner's sugar for dusting

Line a shallow tray or pan (20cm/8in square) with a piece of muslin and dust with a little cornflour. Combine the rose water and cornflour to make a smooth paste and set aside.

In a pan, combine the sugar, water and lemon juice. Bring to the boil, and over a medium heat stir constantly, allowing the sugar to disolve and taking care the mixture doesn't burn.

Add a little of the hot sugar syrup to the rose water and cornflour and mix thoroughly. Remove the pan of sugar syrup from the heat, add the rose water and cornflour mix and whisk thoroughly.

Return to a medium heat, continue to stir until the mixture takes on a clearer appearance and thickens to a jelly type consistency. Remove from the heat; at this point add chopped nuts of your choice (optional).

Pour the mix onto the prepared tray and allow to cool and set, preferably overnight.

Turn out the lokum onto a work surface well dusted with icing sugar. Remove the muslin, cut into squares, dust generously with more icing sugar and serve each square elegantly skewered on a wooden cocktail stick.

Aşure

Noah's pudding of forty ingredients

Undoubtedly, this is Turkey's most famous dessert, and certainly the one most shrouded in myth and tradition. Legend has it, that as the waters of the great flood were subsiding, Noah asked his wife to put together a meal using all the ingredients left on the ark. She is said to have thrown together 40 different ingredients and concocted this protein-rich dessert. Everyone prides themselves on having the most exact recipe, but the truth is, whatever you have in the pantry will do. Traditionally in Turkey, *aşure* is prepared only by women who have a daughter and it is eaten to celebrate the 10th day of the Muslim month Muharrem, the anniversary of the martyrdom of Imam Hüseyin, grandson of Mohammed.

Serves 12
Preparation time - 2 days
Cooking time - 3 hours

1/2 cup dried chickpeas	**10 dried apricots**
1/2 cup dried haricot beans	**grated zest of 1 orange**
1/2 cup dried broad beans	**1 teaspoon vanilla sugar**
3/4 cup whole wheat	**11/2 cups sugar**
1/2 cup rice	**1 cup milk**
1/2 cup sultanas/seedless raisins	**2 tablespoons rose water**
10 dried figs	

For garnish, choose any combination of the following – blanched almonds, hazelnuts, walnuts, ground pistachio nuts, sliced dried figs and apricots, currants, sultanas, desiccated coconut, ground cinnamon and fresh pomegranate seeds.

Soak the chickpeas, haricot and broad beans separately in plenty of water overnight. Put the wheat in a large heavy-based pan with 2 cups of water and bring to the boil. Remove from the heat and leave the wheat in this hot water to soak overnight. (This will dramatically cut down the cooking time the following day).

Drain and cook the pre-soaked chickpeas, haricot and broad beans separately in plenty of fresh water until tender. Drain and reserve the combined cooking liquids. When the chickpeas are cool enough to handle remove their shells.

Rinse the rice and add to the pan of wheat with 6 cups of the reserved cooking liquid. Bring to the boil, cover and simmer on a low heat, stirring frequently, for about 2 hours or until the wheat is tender. If at anytime the mixture appears to be getting too thick and dry, add a little more of the reserved cooking liquid. Meanwhile, soak the dried fruits in hot water for 30 minutes. Drain and finely chop the figs and apricots. Add this fruit and orange zest to the pan of wheat and rice, simmer for a further 5 minutes and then add the cooked chickpeas, haricot and broad beans. Simmer for a further 5 minutes and then add the sugar, vanilla sugar and milk, stirring until the sugar dissolves.

Cook for a further 15 minutes, the consistency should be that of a thin porridge, adding a little more water if required. Remove from the heat and stir in the rose water. Pour into individual dessert bowls or one large one. After a few hours the consistency of the mixture will thicken, and if left overnight, will be perfect.

Serve chilled, garnished with any combination of the suggestions above.

Revani

The poet's semolina sponge soaked in syrup

This dish is named after a 16th Century Turkish poet, who wrote reams extolling the delights of food. Revani is an age-old favourite and revered by many.

Serves 8
Preparation time - 25 minutes
Cooking time - 30 minutes

**60g/20oz plain white flour
120g/4oz fine semolina
6 eggs, separated
120g/4oz sugar
grated zest of 1 orange**

For the syrup -
**juice and grated zest of 2 lemons
1 cup fine sugar
1 1/2 cups water**

To garnish -
**desiccated coconut and
finely ground pistachios**

Preheat oven to 180c/350f/gas mark 4.

Line a cake tin (25cm/10in diameter) with greaseproof paper.

Sift the flour into a bowl and stir in the semolina.

In a larger bowl beat the egg yolks with the sugar until light and creamy. Beat in the orange zest and gradually add the flour and semolina mix.

In another bowl, whisk the egg whites to stiff peaks and fold them into the cake mixture. Spoon it into the prepared cake tin and bake for about 30 minutes until golden brown. To be completely sure the sponge is cooked, test with a wooden toothpick, which should come out clean. Leave to cool slightly and turn the oven down to a minimum heat.

Meanwhile, prepare the syrup by adding all the ingredients to a pan. Bring to the boil and simmer gently for 10 minutes. Set aside to cool.

Whilst the revani is still in the cake tin cut into squares and pour the syrup over. Return to the oven for 10 minutes. Remove and set aside, allowing the sponge to absorb the syrup.

Transfer to a serving dish and sprinkle with the coconut and/or pistachios and serve with kaymak or clotted cream.

Fırında Sütlaç

Oven baked rice pudding

Everyone's favourite, *sütlaç* is just so comforting! It isn't possible to find a pudding shop in Turkey that doesn't have its own unique version. Traditionally puddings don't follow a large meal; more often a visit to the *muhallebici* (pudding shop) is to celebrate a special occasion, and very often a favourite hangout for young sweethearts. As with most Turkish sweets, *sütlaç* is enjoyed cold.

Serves 6
Preparation time - 20 minutes
Cooking time - 1 1/2 hours

1/2 cup short grain rice	**2 egg yolks**
4 cups milk	**1 tablespoon cornflour/cornstarch**
1 cup sugar	**1 teaspoon vanilla sugar**
pinch of salt	**ground cinnamon**
1 tablespoon finely grated orange zest	

Rinse the rice, put in a pan with a cup of water and cook over a low heat until all the water is absorbed and the rice is soft.

Add the milk, sugar, pinch of salt and orange zest to the rice and simmer for a further 15 minutes.

Meanwhile, beat together the egg yolks with the cornflour and a little of the hot milk from the pudding mixture to form a smooth, thin paste. Remove the pan from the heat and stir in the egg and cornflour mixture thoroughly. Return to a low heat and cook for a further 15 minutes to achieve a nice creamy consistency.

Remove from the heat and stir in the vanilla sugar. Pour into individual ovenproof dishes, terracotta bowls are perfect, and set aside until the puddings are set and skin forms on top.

Sprinkle the puddings with ground cinnamon and place the bowls on an oven tray. Pour a little water into the tray and bake in a hot oven until the tops are golden.

Keşkül

Almond milk pudding

From the sacred kitchens of the dervishes, this distinguished milk pudding was named after the special bowls of ebony, or coconut shells in which it was served. Turkey grows some of the best almonds in the world; springtime orchards in bloom are a sight to behold. For the best results, buy shelled almonds and blanch them yourself – cover with boiling water for 30 minutes, then drain and rub away the skins easily.

Serves 6
Preparation time - 20 minutes
Cooking time - 40 minutes

1 cup blanched almonds
4 cups milk
1 cup sugar
2 tablespoons cornflour/cornstarch
2 tablespoons rice flour
1 teaspoon vanilla sugar
pinch salt
1 teaspoon almond essence
(or 1 tablespoon rose water)

For garnish, choose any combination of the following -
ground almonds
ground pistachio nuts
desiccated coconut

In a food processor, grind the almonds with enough water to create a paste. Add to this a cup of milk and pass this mixture through a sieve.

In a bowl, combine the cornflour and rice flour and slowly mix in the almond milk to create a thin, creamy paste.

Over a low heat, slowly bring the remaining 3 cups of milk to the boil. Add the sugar, a pinch of salt and the vanilla sugar and stir until the sugar has dissolved. Remove from the heat. Add a little of the hot milk to the almond mixture, whisk thoroughly and return this mixture to the pan.

Over a low heat, stirring constantly, cook for 15 minutes until the consistency becomes thick and creamy. Remove from the heat and stir in the almond essence or rose water.

Pour into individual serving bowls and refrigerate overnight.

Serve chilled, garnished with any combination of ground nuts and coconut.

Kaymaklı Kayısı Tatlısı

Apricots stuffed with clotted cream

One of Turkey's most prolific fruits is the apricot. Because of their abundance, some of the yearly harvest is allowed to dry in the hot summer sun in order to be enjoyed all year round. Malatya, in southeast Turkey, is particularly famous for excellent dried apricots which are exported throughout the world.

Serves 4 - 6
Preparation time - 10 minutes
Cooking time - 20 minutes

250g/8oz Turkish dried apricots　　　　**4 tablespoons sugar**
1 cup water　　　　**kaymak or clotted cream to serve**
juice of 1/2 lemon　　　　**crushed pistachio nuts for garnish**

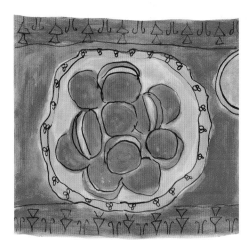

Soak the apricots overnight in cold water. Drain and reserve 1 cup of the water. Put the water in a pan with the apricots, lemon juice and sugar. Boil gently for 10 minutes or until the syrup thickens, taking care not to allow the apricots to become mushy.

Allow to cool, split open the apricots and stuff with a spoonful of cream. Arrange in a serving bowl facing up, spoon over the syrup and sprinkle with the crushed pistachio nuts.

Şekerpare

Almond cakes bathed in syrup

Little round cakes, soaked in syrup and topped with an almond, *şekerpare* is also a colloquial term for a small sweet apricot.

Serves 4 - 6
Preparation time - 20 minutes
Cooking time - 35 minutes

1/2 cup fine sugar
120g/4oz butter
1 egg, beaten
2 cups plain white flour
1/2 teaspoon baking powder
pinch of salt
2 tablespoons fine semolina
blanched almonds
1 egg yolk to glaze

For the syrup -
1 cup water
1 cup sugar
squeeze of lemon juice

Preheat oven to 180c/350f/gas mark 4

In a large bowl, cream together the sugar and butter. Add the beaten egg, sift in the flour, baking powder, a pinch of salt and stir in the semolina. Knead well until the mixture is a smooth paste. With well-oiled hands roll the mixture into walnut size balls. Flatten them slightly and place at intervals on a lightly oiled baking sheet. Make an indentation with your finger in the middle of each one and place an almond in the hollow. Brush with beaten egg yolk and bake for 25-30 minutes until firm and golden in colour.

Put the ingredients for the syrup in a pan and cook on a low heat for 10 minutes.

Take the şekerpare from the oven, pour half the syrup over and return to the oven for 5 more minutes.

Pour the remaining syrup over, and allow to cool and absorb the syrup before serving.

Zerde

Saffron rice dessert scented with rose water

Zerde is of Persian origin – zerd in Persian meaning yellow, the colour of saffron. Saffron, the world's most expensive spice, is made from the dried stigmas of the *crocus salivus*. Only a tiny amount is required to give a wonderful colour and delicate bittersweet flavour to this classic dessert. Saffron has the ability to calm and balance the body and is believed to be an aphrodisiac. Maybe for this reason, *zerde* features regularly at Turkish wedding celebrations.

Serves 6
Preparation time - 20 minutes
Cooking time - 45 minutes

pinch of saffron
2 tablespoons rose water
2 tablespoons rice
4 cups water
1 cup sugar
2 teaspoons arrowroot
For the Garnish -
pine nut kernels, currants and
pomegranate seeds

Soak the saffron in rose water overnight.

Soak the rice in hot water for 30 minutes, drain and rinse under cold running water. Cook the rice in 4 cups of water until tender but not mushy. Add the rose water with the saffron and the sugar and continue to boil until the sugar has dissolved. Remove from the heat. Mix the arrowroot thoroughly with 2 tablespoons of cold water and add this to the pan. Return to a low heat and stir continuously until the mixture thickens.

Divide the mixture into 6 small glass bowls and refrigerate.

To serve, garnish with pine nuts, currants and fresh pomegranate seeds.

Hoşmerim

Something nice for my brave man

This dessert originates from central Anatolia and allegedly was made to satisfy a man who came home after a long absence from his village. Using ingredients from the pantry, his wife concocted a dessert which romantically conjured up the true meaning of home for him. There are many variations; this is one of the most interesting.

Serves 6
Preparation time - 10 minutes
Cooking time - 40 minutes

450g/1lb soft white Turkish cheese
2 tablespoons plain white flour
1 cup sugar
4 tablespoons shelled walnuts, chopped
2 tablespoons raisins
pekmez (grape syrup) to serve

Mash the cheese with a fork. Put in a pan and stir over a low heat until it starts to melt.

In a separate pan, and over a low heat, stir the flour until it turns a golden beige colour.

Reserving a little of the sugar for the topping, stir the remainder into the melted cheese and cook for 1 minute. Add to this the flour and cook until the mixture thickens. Remove from the heat and stir in the walnuts and raisins.

Spread out in a buttered oven dish, sprinkle the reserved sugar over and bake in a moderately hot oven for about 30 minutes or until the top has a golden crust.

Serve at room temperature drizzled with pekmez.

Note – It takes 2.5kg/5lbs of fresh grapes to produce 450g/1lb of dried raisins, sultanas or currants. In the grape growing regions of Anatolia, surplus grapes are boiled in huge cauldrons to produce pekmez – concentrated grape syrup. This is then stored and used through the winter months as a sweetening agent.

Ayva Tatlısı

Quince dessert

Quinces are very versatile, make great preserves, can be added to meat dishes or used to make this dramatically red dessert. The red colour comes from the pectin in the seeds, which are included during the cooking procedure. Serve with kaymak or clotted cream.

Serves 4 - 6
Preparation time - 10 minutes
Cooking time - 60 minutes

4 quinces
8 cloves
1 cup water
1 cup sugar
juice of 1/2 lemon
kaymak/clotted cream

Peel the quinces and cut in half. Reserving the seeds, scoop out the cores to create hollows, and insert a clove into each one. Place the quinces in a pan able to accommodate them in one layer. Add the water, seeds, sugar and lemon juice.

Cook over a low heat for about 60 minutes or until the fruit is tender, pink and slightly caramelised. If needed add a little extra water during cooking time to prevent the fruit sticking to the bottom of the pan.

Leave to cool in the pan, remove the cloves and seeds if you wish and serve with a dollop of cream in the hollow of the fruit.

Note - Quinces are rich in soluble fibre and pectin and therefore ideal for jams and jellies.

Gül Sulu Muhallebi

Milk pudding scented with rose water

This is the original pudding shop recipe and is traditionally served with rose water and icing sugar. If you prefer, it can be served with cinnamon, grated coconut, cocoa or even *pekmez* (grape syrup).

Serves 4 - 6
Preparation time - 10 minutes
Cooking time - 30 minutes

3 tablespoons rice flour
2 tablespoons cornflour/cornstarch
4 cups milk
3 tablespoons sugar
pinch salt
rose water
icing sugar/confectioner's sugar

Put the rice flour and cornflour in a bowl. Add a little of the milk and whisk together to make a smooth paste. Put the rest of the milk, sugar and a pinch of salt in a pan and bring to the boil slowly to ensure the sugar dissolves.

Add the hot milk slowly to the flour paste. Beat together thoroughly and return to the pan. Heat gently, stirring constantly, and cook until the mixture thickens. Pour into individual bowls or a mould and allow to cool and a skin to form. Refrigerate.

Serve sprinkled with rose water and dusted with icing sugar.

Saray Lokması

Palace fritters soaked in syrup

Lokma are little dough balls the size of ping-pong balls, deep-fried and smothered in syrup. They are believed to represent the Prophet Mohammed's seal and they are prepared in huge quantity during the religious Kandil celebrations. Along with *helva* it can be made on the 7th, 40th and 52nd day to commemorate the loss of a loved one, and distributed to friends, neighbours, and the poor.

Serves 10
Preparation time - 60 minutes
Cooking time - 10 minutes

2 teaspoons dried yeast
2 teaspoons sugar
1 cup lukewarm water
2 cups of plain white flour
1 teaspoon cinnamon
pinch salt
sunflower oil for deep frying

For the syrup -
1 cup water
2 cups sugar
1 tablespoon lemon juice

Mix the yeast with the sugar and add half the lukewarm water. Sift the flour, cinnamon and salt into a bowl, make a well in the middle and pour in the yeast mix. Combine the flour to make a batter, cover and leave for 20 minutes. Add the rest of the lukewarm water and mix everything together to make a smooth dough. Cover and leave to prove in a warm place until double its size.

Put the ingredients for the syrup into a pan and boil gently for 10 minutes. Set aside to cool.

Heat the sunflower oil in a deep pan and, using a wet teaspoon, drop small amounts of the dough into the oil, constantly wetting the spoon in a bowl of water to prevent the dough sticking to the spoon. Take care not to overload the pan and using a straining spoon, stir to ensure the balls cook evenly. Remove when golden brown and drain on absorbent kitchen paper.

Toss the fritters in the syrup and serve immediately.

Tavuk Göğsü Kazandibi

Caramelised chicken breast cream pudding

This can be said to be one of Turkey's most unusual milk puddings. It was inherited from the Romans by the Turks and the French, and is the authentic blancmange, mysteriously enough, now almost lost in French cuisine. It is made with chicken breast meat. The chicken is used to provide texture and nutrition to the dessert, but the flavour and texture of chicken is not detectable. *Kazandibi* literally means bottom of the cauldron and refers to the burnt caramelised appearance of the dessert.

Serves 4 - 6
Preparation time - 10 minutes
Cooking time - 1 hour

1/2 chicken breast
3 cups milk
6 tablespoons sugar
2 tablespoons rice flour
1 tablespoon cornflour/corn starch
butter
ground cinnamon
icing sugar/confectioner's sugar

Place the chicken breast in a pan, cover with water and cook gently for 1 hour. Drain and leave to cool.

Shred the chicken, place in a bowl and cover with cold water.

Place the sugar, rice flour and cornflour in a pan and gradually whisk in some of the milk to create a paste. Add the rest of the milk, heat through gently and continue whisking until the mixture thickens. Simmer gently for 10 minutes and set aside.

Crumble the chicken in the water. Place in a sieve and rinse under running cold water. Push the chicken in the sieve with the back of a wooden spoon until it is a mushy pulp. Add the chicken to the thickened pudding mix and return to the heat. Stir well and cook gently for another 10 minutes.

Grease a baking tray with butter and dust with icing sugar. Slowly pour the hot chicken pudding mixture over it and smooth out with a wooden spoon. The mixture should not be more than 2cm/1/4 in thick. Place the tray over a high heat and move back and forth to caramelise the underside of the pudding. When the edges turn golden and it starts to curl up, it is done. Leave to cool and then refrigerate.

To serve, cut the slightly hardened pudding into squares and gently lift from the tray with a spatula. Arrange on separate plates curled up in a roll exposing the caramelised coating. Dust with cinnamon and garnish with mint leaves, slices of fruit or whole strawberries.

Kabak Tatlısı

Winter pumpkin dessert

Luscious bright orange pumpkin prepared this way warms up any winter evening. In Turkey, the seeds of the pumpkin are never discarded but oven-roasted with salt to nibble on through the winter months, very nutritious and a huge Anatolian pastime!

Serves 6
Preparation time - 10 minutes
Cooking time - 40 minutes

1kg/2lbs peeled pumpkin
1 cup sugar
juice of 1/2 lemon
1 cup water
crushed walnuts to garnish
kaymak/clotted cream to serve

Cut the pumpkin into manageable wedges. Place in a broad-based pan in layers, sprinkling sugar between the layers. Add the lemon juice and water and cook on a low heat until the pumpkin is tender and most of the liquid is absorbed. Add a little more water if required during cooking time to prevent the fruit sticking to the bottom of the pan.

Leave to cool in the pan.

Serve sprinkled with the crushed walnuts and accompanied with a dollop of cream.

Hanım Göbeği

Ladies' belly buttons in syrup

Visions of the harem, this is one of the erotically named sweets to adorn the sultan's table. Use this recipe and roll into small log shapes to make *vezir parmağı* (Vizier's fingers) or make a ball, flatten in the palm of your hand and then fold in two to form *dilber dudağı* (sweetheart's lips).

Serves 6
Preparation time - 30 minutes
Cooking time - 20 minutes

1 1/2 cups water
6 tablespoons butter
1 teaspoon sugar
pinch salt
1 tablespoon semolina
1 cup plain white flour, sifted
3 eggs, beaten
sunflower oil for deep frying

For the syrup -
1 cup water
1 cup sugar
squeeze of lemon juice

Put the water, butter, sugar and salt in a pan, heat and bring to the boil. Remove from the heat and gradually add the semolina and sifted flour. Return the pan to a low heat and cook slowly, combining the ingredients thoroughly until the mixture leaves the side of the pan. Remove from the heat and set aside to cool slightly. Beat in the eggs and refrigerate for 30 minutes.

Put the ingredients for the syrup in a pan and on a low heat simmer for 10 minutes. Set aside to cool.

Heat the sunflower oil in a deep pan. With well-oiled hands take spoonfuls of the dough the size of a large walnut, roll into balls, flatten slightly and make an indentation with your forefinger to create the belly button. Take care not to overload the pan and that the oil doesn't get too hot. Fry until puffed up and golden brown. Remove with a straining spoon and drain on absorbent kitchen paper.

Serve soaked in the syrup.

Vişneli Ekmek Tatlısı

Sour cherry bread dessert

In the summer time Turkey's orchards yield an abundant range of mouthwatering fruits. Cherries are native to Anatolia and plentiful. This recipe is a fantastic way to use up old bread to make a delicious and dramatically colourful dessert. It is perfectly accompanied with *kaymak*, Turkey's wonderful thick clotted cream made from the milk of water buffalos.

Serves 6
Preparation time - 30 minutes

**500g/1lb fresh large Morello cherries
(stones removed)
8 slices stale white bread
(crusts removed)**

**1/2 cup sugar
squeeze of lemon juice
mint leaves to decorate
kaymak/clotted cream to serve**

Put the cherries in a pan with the sugar and 2 cups of water. Bring to the boil and simmer gently for 10 minutes. Remove from the heat. Strain through a sieve into another pan and put the fruit to one side. Return the juice to the heat, add a squeeze of lemon juice and continue simmering until slightly thickened. Check for sweetness and add a little more sugar if required.

Bake the slices of bread lightly in the oven. Arrange 4 slices of bread in the bottom of a square serving dish. Pour half the juice over and half the cherries. Add a second layer of bread and pour the remaining juice and cherries over.

Set aside to cool and allow all the juice to be absorbed. Refrigerate until required.

To serve, cut into portions and serve each portion decorated with a mint leaf and a dollop of kaymak or clotted cream.

Note – Cherries stimulate and cleanse the system, removing toxins from the kidneys. Canned or conserve cherries can be used if fresh sour cherries are difficult to come by.

Bülbül Yuvası

Nightingales' nests of walnuts and syrup

There are many types of *baklava*. This recipe is reasonably easy and uses pre-packaged readily available filo pastry. Each sheet of pastry is rolled up with nuts, coiled in a nest shape and smothered in syrup.

Serves 6
Preparation time - 30 minutes
Cooking time - 30 minutes

2 cups sugar	**2 cups finely ground walnuts**
1 1/2 cups water	**1 tablespoon sugar**
1 tablespoon lemon juice	**1 teaspoon cinnamon**
12 sheets of filo pastry	**1/4 cup ground pistachio nuts for garnish**
1 cup melted butter	

Preheat oven to 180c/350f/gas mark 4.

To make the syrup, place the sugar and water in a pan and simmer over a low heat for 10 minutes. Add the lemon juice, heat through and then remove from the heat. Set aside to cool.

Mix together the walnuts, sugar and cinnamon and set aside. Using some of the melted butter, grease a baking sheet.

Working with one sheet of filo at a time, and keeping the longest edge of the pastry facing you, brush with melted butter and sprinkle some ground walnut mixture over. Roll up the pastry away from you creating a wrinkled tube. Starting at one end, coil the rolled up tube around itself and wind into a spiral to resemble a nest. Continue in the same way with the rest of the pastry.

Place the nests quite tightly packed together on the baking sheet, making sure the ends are tucked under to prevent the filling escaping. Brush well with more melted butter and bake in the preheated oven for about 30 minutes or until golden brown.

Pour half the cooled syrup over the baked nests and return to the oven for a further 5 minutes.

Pour the remaining syrup over, allowing the nests to soak it up as they cool.

Sprinkle with a garnish of ground pistachio nuts to serve.

Note – While working, always keep filo pastry covered with a damp cloth to prevent it drying out and becoming difficult to manage.

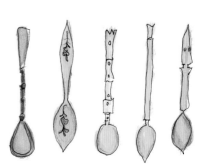

İncir Tatlısı

Poached figs stuffed with walnuts and clotted cream

In Turkey, August is the month of the fig. They grow in huge quantities and are consumed with gusto. In the Mediterranean and Aegean regions the roadsides are flanked by children offering them to passing motorists. Figs that don't make it to the table in their fresh form are dried in the hot summer sun and are transformed into a luscious dried variety to be enjoyed the whole year round.

Serves 6
Preparation time - 15 minutes
Cook time - 10 minutes

500g/1lb Turkish dried figs
2 tablespoons sugar
juice of 1/2 lemon
50g/2oz shelled walnuts
kaymak/clotted cream

Place the figs to soak in hot water for 1 hour and then gently simmer in the same water until they are soft but not mushy.

Drain and pass the cooking liquid through a sieve into another pan. Add the sugar and lemon juice to the cooking liquid. Continue cooking gently to create concentrated fig syrup. Set aside to cool.

When cool enough to handle gently split open the figs. Gently spoon in some kaymak and pop in a walnut.

Serve drizzled with the fig syrup.

Note – Figs are an excellent source of calcium.

Künefe

Syrup soaked, cheese filled pastry strands

Tel *kadayıf* is dough pushed through a sieve to form delicate strands, which looks like vermicelli and when soaked in butter and baked resembles golden shredded wheat. It is the basis for many desserts but this is the most impressive. The hot cheese should ooze out giving an interesting contrast to the syrup-soaked, crunchy casing. Any unsalted cheese which melts easily can be used – mozzarella works well. It can be baked in one big pan or smaller ones as individual portions.

Serves 8
Preparation time - 20 minutes
Cooking time - 30 minutes

2 cups sugar
1 1/2 cups water
1 tablespoon lemon juice
500g/1lb tel kadayıf (pastry strands)
1 cup melted butter
500g/1lb unsalted cheese, grated
1/2 cup ground pistachio nuts for garnish

Preheat oven to 180c/350f/gas mark 4.

To make the syrup, place the sugar and water in a pan and simmer over a low heat for 10 minutes. Add the lemon juice, heat through and then remove from the heat. Set aside to cool.

Using some of the melted butter, grease 8 small ovenproof metal dishes or one large one.

Soak the pastry strands well in the melted butter. Use more butter if necessary, as it is important that it is well soaked in order to prevent it burning during the baking time. Divide the pastry strands in two. From one half, line the dishes to be used. Sprinkle the grated cheese evenly over and then cover with the remaining strands.

Bake in the preheated oven for 30 minutes or until the strands are a deep golden colour.

Serve immediately whilst still hot and the cheese gooey, drenched in the prepared syrup and with a sprinkling of ground pistachio nuts.

Index

Index

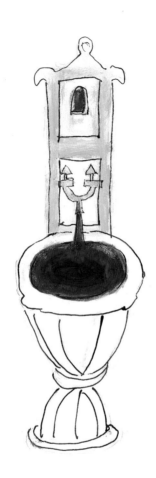